Words

JEAN-PAUL SARTRE

TRANSLATED BY
IRENE CLEPHANE

PENGUIN BOOKS

IN ASSOCIATION WITH
HAMISH HAMILTON

Penguin Books Ltd, Harmondsworth, Middlesex, England
Viking Penguin Inc., 40 West 23rd Street, New York, New York 10010, U.S.A.
Penguin Books Australia Ltd, Ringwood, Victoria, Australia
Penguin Books Canada Limited, 2801 John Street, Markham, Ontario, Canada L3R 1B4
Penguin Books (N.Z.) Ltd, 182–190 Wairau Road, Auckland 10, New Zealand

—

Les Mots first published in France 1964
This translation published by Hamish Hamilton 1964
Published in Penguin Books 1967
Reprinted 1969, 1971, 1972, 1974, 1976, 1977, 1979,
1981, 1983, 1985, 1986

—

—

Set, printed and bound in Great Britain by
Cox & Wyman Ltd, Reading
Set in Monotype Garamond

TO MADAME Z

PART ONE

*

READING

IN Alsace, round about 1850, a schoolmaster, burdened with children, agreed to become a grocer. But he wanted some compensation for unfrocking himself: since he had given up forming minds, one of his sons would form souls; there would be a pastor in the family, and it would be Charles. Charles ran off, preferring to pursue a bareback rider. His portrait was turned to the wall and all mention of his name was forbidden. Whose turn next? Auguste, the second son, hastily copied his father's sacrifice: he went into trade and did well at it. That left Louis, who showed no special aptitude: the father grabbed this quiet son and, in a flash, made a minister of him. Then Louis carried obedience a stage further by himself begetting a minister, Albert Schweitzer, whose career is well known. In the meantime, Charles had not caught up with his bareback rider; his father's grand gesture had left its mark on him; all his life, he preserved a taste for the sublime and turned his energies to elevating trivial incidents into great occasions. He did not dream, as will be seen, of avoiding the family vocation: he hoped to dedicate himself to an attenuated form of spirituality, a priesthood which would allow him bareback riders. The answer lay in teaching: Charles decided to teach German. He passed an oral examination on a thesis about Hans Sachs, settled for the direct method, which he later claimed to have invented, published, in collaboration with Monsieur Simonnot, a highly-regarded *Deutsches Lesebuch*, and enjoyed a rapid career: Mâcon, Lyons, and Paris. At a prize-giving day in Paris, he made a speech which was honoured with a separate off-print: 'Monsieur le Ministre, Mesdames, Messieurs, my dear children, you'll never guess what I am going to talk to you about today! About music!' He was very good at occasional verse. At family reunions, he used to say: 'Louis is the most religious and Auguste the richest; I am the most intelligent.' The brothers would laugh and the sisters-in-law would purse

9

their lips. In Mâcon, Charles Schweitzer had married Louise Guillemin, daughter of a Catholic lawyer. She loathed her honeymoon: he had torn her away before the end of the meal and flung her into a train. At seventy, Louise still used to tell about the leek salad they had been given in a railway refreshment room: 'He took all the white bits and left me the green.' They spent a fortnight in Alsace without leaving the table; the brothers told each other scatological stories in dialect; now and then, the pastor would turn to Louise and translate them, out of Christian charity. It was not long before she produced good enough reasons to exempt her from all conjugal intercourse and to give her the right to a bedroom on her own; she would speak of her migraine, take to her bed, and began to hate noise, passion and enthusiasm, all the shabby vulgarity and theatricality of life with the Schweitzers. This sharp-tongued, lively, cold woman had clear but wrong opinions, because her husband had right but muddled ones. Because he was credulous and a liar, she suspected everything: 'They make out that the world goes round; what do they know about it?' Surrounded by virtuous play-actors, she came to hate both play-acting and virtue. This very subtle realist, stranded in a family of crude believers, became, through defiance, a disciple of Voltaire without having read him. Delicate and plump, cynical and vivacious, she became a force of pure negation; with a lift of her eyebrows and an imperceptible smile, she would reduce all grandiose attitudes to rubble, to please herself and without anyone's noticing. Her negative pride and selfish love of denial devoured her. She did not see anyone, because she was too proud to covet first place and too vain to accept the second. 'Learn,' she used to say, 'how to make yourself desired.' She was greatly desired, then less and less and, as she was not seen, she was eventually forgotten. From then on, she hardly ever left her armchair or her bed. Creatures of nature and puritans – a combination of virtues less rare than people think – the Schweitzers loved coarse words which, while they minimized the body in true Christian fashion, manifested their willing acceptance of the natural functions; Louise liked euphemisms. She used to read a lot of suggestive stories whose plots inter-

ested her less than the transparent veils which wrapped them: 'It's daring, it's well written,' she used to say with an air of delicacy. '*Glissez, mortels, n'appuyez pas!*'* This woman of ice thought she would die of laughter when she read Adolphe Belot's *La Fille de feu*. She loved telling stories about wedding nights which always ended in disaster; sometimes the husband, in his brutal haste, would break his wife's neck against the wooden bed; sometimes the young bride would be found, next morning, sheltering in the wardrobe, naked and mad. Louise lived in semi-darkness; when Charles went into her room and flung back the shutters or lit all the lamps, she would put her hands to her eyes and moan: 'Charles! you're blinding me!' But her powers of resistance did not go beyond the bounds of temperamental opposition: Charles inspired her with fear, a good deal of annoyance, and sometimes with friendship, too, provided he did not touch her. She gave in to him over everything as soon as he began to shout. He sprung four children on her: a daughter who died in infancy, two sons and another daughter. Through either indifference or deference, he allowed them to be brought up in the Catholic religion. Though an unbeliever, Louise made them believers through hatred of Protestantism. The two boys took their mother's side; she gently alienated them from their overbearing father; Charles did not even notice. The elder, Georges, went to the École Polytechnique; the second son, Émile, became a teacher of German. He fascinates me: I know that he remained a bachelor but that he imitated his father in every way, even though he did not like him. Father and son quarrelled in the end; there were some memorable reconciliations. Émile hid his life; he adored his mother and, up to the end, used to visit her secretly, without any warning; he would smother her with hugs and kisses, start talking about his father, ironically at first, then angrily, and leave her, with a slam of the door. I think she loved him, but he frightened her: these two uncouth, difficult men wore her out and she preferred Georges who was never there. Émile died in 1927, crazed with loneliness: a revolver was found under his pillow; a hundred pairs of

* From a poem by Pierre-Charles Roy (1683–1764).

socks in holes and twenty pairs of down-at-heel shoes in his trunks.

Anne-Marie, the younger daughter, spent her childhood on a chair. She was taught to be bored, to hold herself straight, and to sew. She had gifts: it was thought refined to let them lie fallow; she had brilliance: it was carefully kept from her. These modest yet proud middle-class people considered beauty above their means or below their condition; they allowed it to titled women and prostitutes. Louise had the barrenest of prides; afraid of being taken in, she denied the most obvious qualities in her children, her husband, and herself. Charles had no idea how to recognize beauty in others: he confused it with health: after his wife's illness, he took consolation in robust, ruddy-complexioned idealists with moustaches who were always well. Fifty years later, turning the pages of a family album, Anne-Marie realized that she had been beautiful.

Just about the same time that Charles Schweitzer met Louise Guillemin, a country doctor married the daughter of a rich Périgord landowner and settled with her in the gloomy main street of Thiviers, opposite the chemist's shop. The day after the wedding, it came out that the father-in-law was penniless. Disgusted, Doctor Sartre did not speak to his wife for forty years; at meals, he communicated by signs, and in the end she used to refer to him as 'my lodger'. Yet he shared her bed and from time to time, without a word, got her with child: she gave him two sons and a daughter; these children of silence were called Jean-Baptiste, Joseph, and Hélène. Hélène married late in years a cavalry officer who went mad; Joseph did his military service in the Zouaves and retired early to his parents' home. He had no profession: trapped between the silence of the one and the scolding of the other, he developed a stammer and spent his life struggling for words. Jean-Baptiste wanted to study for the Navy and see the sea. At Cherbourg in 1904, as a naval officer, his health already undermined by the fevers of Cochin-China, he met Anne-Marie Schweitzer, seized on this tall, neglected girl, married her, gave her a child with all speed, myself, and tried to seek refuge in death.

Dying is not easy: the fever in his entrails increased gradually, with occasional remissions. Anne-Marie looked after him devotedly though she did not carry indecency so far as to love him. Louise had warned her against married life: after the blood wedding, it meant an endless chain of sacrifices, broken by nights of coarseness. Following her mother's example, my mother preferred duty to pleasure. She did not know my father very well, either before or after their marriage, and she must sometimes have wondered why this stranger had resolved to die in her arms. He was taken to a small farm a few miles outside Thiviers; his father used to come and visit him each day by trap. Nights of vigil and worry exhausted Anne-Marie and her milk dried up; I was sent to a wet-nurse not far away and I did my best to die, too: from enteritis and perhaps from resentment. At the age of twenty, my mother, with neither experience nor advice, tore herself away from two dying strangers; her marriage of convenience found its truth in sickness and mourning. Personally, I benefited from the situation: at the time, mothers breast-fed their own children and for a long while; without the fortune of this twin death-agony, I should have been exposed to the difficulties of a late weaning. A sickly child, forcibly weaned at nine months, I was prevented by fever and exhaustion from feeling the last snip of the scissors which severs the bond between mother and child; I plunged into a confused world, peopled with simple hallucinations and worn idols. On my father's death, Anne-Marie and I woke from a common nightmare: I was cured. But we were the victims of a misunderstanding: she lovingly rejoined a son whom she had never really left; I regained consciousness on the lap of a stranger.

Penniless and jobless, Anne-Marie decided to go back to live with her parents. But the insolence of my father's death had offended the Schweitzers: it looked uncommonly like a repudiation. Because she had been unable to foresee it or warn them about it, my mother was held guilty: in her carelessness, she had taken a husband who had not done the accepted things. Everyone acted impeccably towards the tall Ariadne who returned to Meudon with a child in her arms; my grandfather had applied to retire, but he went back to work without a word

13

of reproach; my grandmother enjoyed a quiet triumph. But Anne-Marie, chilled by gratitude, sensed the blame beneath their decency: families naturally prefer widows to unmarried mothers, but only just. To earn her forgiveness, she gave herself unsparingly, kept house for her parents, at Meudon and then in Paris, became governess, nurse, majordomo, lady's companion and maid, without being able to dispel her mother's unspoken annoyance. Louise found it irksome to compile the menu every morning and do the accounts every evening, but she did not like them to be done for her; she let herself be relieved of her obligations and at the same time resented the loss of her prerogatives. This ageing, cynical woman had only one illusion: she thought she was indispensable. The illusion faded: Louise began to feel jealous of her daughter. Poor Anne-Marie: passive, she would have been accused of being a burden; active, she was suspected of wanting to boss the household. To avoid the first reef took all her courage; to avoid the second, all her humility. It was not long before the young widow became a minor again: a virgin tarnished. She was not refused pocket-money: they forgot to give her any; she wore her clothes to a thread and it never occurred to my grandfather to renew them. She was barely permitted to go out alone. When her old friends, most of them married, invited her to supper, she had to ask permission well in advance and promise that she would be brought back before ten. Halfway through the meal, the head of the family would get up from the table to drive her home. Meanwhile, my grandfather, in his nightshirt, would be patrolling his bedroom, watch in hand. On the final stroke of ten, he would begin to roar. Invitations grew rare, and my mother came to dislike such costly pleasures.

Jean-Baptiste's death was the great event of my life: it returned my mother to her chains and it gave me my freedom.

The rule is that there are no good fathers; it is not the men who are at fault but the paternal bond which is rotten. There is nothing better than to produce children, but what a sin to *have* some! If he had lived, my father would have lain down on

14

me and crushed me. Fortunately, he died young; among the Aeneases each carrying his Anchises on his shoulders, I cross from one bank to the other, alone, detesting those invisible fathers who ride piggy-back on their sons throughout their lives; I left behind me a dead young man who did not have time to be my father and who could, today, be my son. Was it a good or a bad thing? I do not know; but I am happy to subscribe to the judgement of an eminent psychoanalyst: I have no Super-Ego.

Dying is not everything: you have to die in time. Later on, I felt guilty; a sensitive orphan blames himself: his parents, offended by the sight of him, have retired to their flats in the sky. But I was delighted: my unhappy condition imposed respect and established my importance; I numbered my mourning among my virtues. My father had been gracious enough to die in the wrong: my grandmother kept saying that he had shirked his responsibilities; my grandfather, rightly proud of the Schweitzers' longevity, refused to admit that a man could pass away at thirty; in the light of this suspect death, he came to doubt if his son-in-law had ever existed and, in the end, he forgot him. I did not even have to forget him; by taking French leave, Jean-Baptiste had denied me the pleasure of meeting him. Even today, I am amazed how little I know about him. Yet he loved, he wanted to live and he saw himself dying; that is enough to make up a whole man. But no one in the family has been able to rouse my curiosity about him. For some years, I saw, over my bed, the portrait of a junior officer with frank eyes, a round, balding head and a heavy moustache: when my mother remarried, the portrait disappeared. Later, I inherited some books of his: a work by Le Dantec on the future of science, and another by Weber entitled: *Vers le positivisme par l'idéalisme absolu.* Like all his contemporaries, he read rubbish. In the margins, I found some indecipherable scribbles, the remains of a small light which lived and flickered about the time of my birth. I sold the books: the dead man meant so little to me. I know him by hearsay, like the Man in the Iron Mask or the Chevalier d'Éon, and what I know about him does not relate to me: no one remembers if he loved me, if he took me in his arms or if he looked at his son with his clear eyes, now eaten away: these are lost emotions. This father is not even a ghost, not even a glance: both of us dwelt for some time on the same earth, that is all. It was conveyed to me that I was the child of a miracle rather than a dead man's son. Hence, without any doubt, my incredible levity. I am not a leader and I do not aspire to be one. Giving orders and obeying them are one and the same thing. Even the most authoritarian gives orders in someone else's name, some holy parasite – his father – and passes on the abstract violences he himself accepts. I have never in my life given an order without laughing or making others laugh; the fact is that I am not eaten up by the canker of power: I have not been taught obedience.

Whom should I have obeyed? I was shown a young giantess, and I was told that she was my mother. On my own, I should more likely have taken her for an elder sister. This virgin, who lived with us, watched and domineered over by everyone, was there to wait on me. I loved her: but how could I respect her if no one else did? There were three bedrooms in our house: my grandfather's, my grandmother's, and the "children's". We were the 'children': both minors and both maintained. But I was the one who was considered. A young girl's bed had been put into *my* room. The young girl slept alone and woke chaste: I would still be asleep when she ran and took her 'tub' in the bathroom; she would come back fully dressed: how could she have given birth to me? She would tell me her troubles and I would listen sympathetically: I should marry her later on so as to look after her. I promised her I would protect her and devote my young importance to her service. Did they think I would obey her? I was kind enough to give in to her entreaties. Besides, she did not give me any orders: she would sketch in a few light words the future which she praised me for wanting to achieve: 'My little darling is going to be very sweet, very good, he'll let me put the nice drops in his nose.' I allowed myself to be trapped by these soft prophecies.

That left the patriarch: he looked so much like God the Father that he was often taken for him. One day, he entered a church through the vestry; the parish priest was threatening the fainthearted with celestial thunder: 'God is here! He is watching you!' Suddenly the worshippers saw, beneath the pulpit, a tall old man with a beard looking at them: they fled. On other occasions, my grandfather said that they flung themselves at his feet. He developed a taste for such appearances. In September 1914, he appeared in a cinema at Arcachon: we were in the circle, my mother and I, when he called for light; some other men round him were acting as angels and shouting: 'Victory! Victory!' God climbed on to the stage and read the communiqué from the Marne. While his beard was still black, he had been Jehovah, and I suspect it was because of him that Émile died, indirectly. This God of wrath gorged himself on his son's blood. But I turned up at the end of his long life, when his beard had turned white, tobacco had stained it yellow and paternity had ceased to amuse him. Yet if he had begotten me, I feel sure he would not have scrupled to enslave me: out of habit. I was lucky to belong to a dead man: a dead man had poured out the few drops of sperm which are the normal price of a child; I was a fief of the sun and my grandfather could enjoy me without owning me: I was his 'wonder' because he wanted to end his days as a wonder-struck old man; he decided to regard me as an unusual boon from fate, as a free gift which could always be revoked; what could he have demanded of me? My very presence satisfied him. He was the God of Love with the Father's beard and the Son's Sacred Heart; he would lay his hands on me, I would feel the warmth of his palms on my head, he would call me his little one in a voice bleating with affection, and tears would fill his cold eyes. Everyone would exclaim: 'The rascal has turned his head!' It was obvious that he adored me. Did he love me? I find it hard to tell sincerity from artifice in so public an emotion: I do not think he showed much affection for his other grandsons; it is true that he hardly ever saw them and that they had no need of him. But I depended on him for everything: he adored, in me, his generosity.

In fact, he rather overdid the sublime: he was a nineteenth-century man who, like so many others, including Victor Hugo himself, thought he was Victor Hugo. I see this handsome man with his flowing beard, for ever between two melo-dramatic effects, like an alcoholic between two drinks, as the victim of two recently discovered techniques: the art of photo-graphy and 'the art of being a grandfather'.* He had the good and ill fortune to be photogenic; photographs of him filled the house: since there was no such thing as rapid exposure, he had acquired a taste for posing and holding his poses; everything was an excuse to freeze a gesture, to adopt a noble stance or to turn to stone; he relished those brief moments of eternity when he became his own statue. Because of this love of his for taking up a pose, my memories of him are like stiff magic-lantern pictures. Some bushes and myself at the age of five sitting on a tree-trunk: Charles Schweitzer is wearing a panama hat, a cream flannel suit with black stripes, and a white piqué waist-coat, with a watch-chain across it: his pince-nez is dangling at the end of a cord; he is bending over me, his gold-ringed finger in the air, talking. Everything is dark and dank, except his sunlike beard: he is wearing his halo round his chin. I do not know what he is saying: I was too busy listening to hear. I suppose this old Empire republican was teaching me my duties as a citizen and recounting the bourgeois version of history; there had been kings and emperors and they were very wicked; they had been thrown out and everything would be all right. In the evening, when we went to wait for him in the road we would soon spot him, in the crowd of travellers leaving the funicular railway, because of his great height and his dancing-master's walk. However far off he saw us, he used to 'strike an attitude', as if at the behest of some invisible photographer: his beard to windward, his body erect, his feet at right angles, his chest out and his arms spread wide. At this signal, I used to freeze, lean forward; I was the sprinter about to take off, the little bird that pops out of the camera; we would remain a few seconds, face to face, a pretty group in porcelain, then I would dash forward, laden with fruit and flowers and, to my grand-father's joy, rush up to his knees, pretending to be out of breath; he would lift me up off the ground, raise me at arms' length to the skies, then clutch me to his heart murmuring: 'My

* *L'Art d'être grandpère* is the title of a book by Victor Hugo.

18

darling child!' This was the second position, closely watched by the passers-by. We would act out a complete play of a hundred different sketches: flirtations, speedily resolved misunderstandings, good-natured teasings and gentle scoldings, loving resentments, affectionate secrets and passion; we would think up obstacles to our love for the pleasure of brushing them aside: sometimes I would be imperious but my whims could not disguise my exquisite sensibility; he would reveal the sublime and straightforward vanity that becomes grandfathers, and the blindness and the blameworthy weaknesses recommended by Hugo. If I had been put on dry bread, 'he would have brought me jam';* but the two intimidated women were careful to avoid that. And then I was a good child: I found my part so becoming that I could not drop it. In fact, my father's hasty retreat had conferred on me a very incomplete Oedipus complex: no Super-Ego, I agree, but no aggression, either. My mother was mine and no one challenged my quiet possession. I knew nothing of violence and hatred and I was spared the harsh apprenticeship of jealousy; I did not bump myself on its corners, so I distinguished reality at first only by its cheerful inconsistency. Against whom or what could I have rebelled? No one else's whim ever claimed to be my law.

I graciously allowed my shoes to be put on, drops to be put in my nose, and myself to be washed and brushed, dressed and undressed, spruced up and rubbed down. Nothing amused me more than to play at being good. I did not cry, I seldom laughed and I did not make a noise; at four, I was caught putting salt in the jam: out of scientific interest rather than devilment, I suppose; anyway, it is the only crime I can remember. On Sundays the ladies sometimes went to Mass, to hear some good music or a well-known organist: neither of them was a practising Catholic, but the faith of others helped them to ecstatic enjoyment of the music. They believed in God just long enough to enjoy a toccata. I revelled in these moments of lofty spirituality: everyone seemed to be asleep and it was an opportunity for me to do my act: kneeling at my prie-dieu, I would turn into a statue; I must not move even a toe; I would

* Quotation from Hugo's *L'Art d'être grandpère*.

stare straight in front of me, without blinking, until the tears rolled down my cheeks; of course, I would wage a titanic struggle against pins and needles, but I was sure to triumph, so conscious of my strength that I did not hesitate to think up the wickedest temptations for the sheer pleasure of resisting them: supposing I got up and shouted: 'Badaboum!'? Supposing I climbed up the pillar and did wee-wees in the font? These terrifying evocations added greater value, soon afterwards, to my mother's congratulations. But I was lying to myself; I pretended to be in danger so as to add to my glory: the temptations did not intoxicate me for a second; I was far too afraid of a scandal; if I wished to astonish people, it was through my virtues. These facile victories convinced me that I was naturally good; all I had to do was act naturally and I would be heaped with praise. Wicked thoughts and desires, when there were any, came from outside; they were no sooner in me than they sickened and faded away: I was stony ground for evil. Playing at virtue, I never forced or constrained myself: I invented. I enjoyed the princely freedom of an actor who holds the audience in suspense and improves on his own performance. I was adored, therefore I was adorable. Since the world was well-designed, what could have been simpler? I was told that I was good-looking and I believed it. For some time, I had had a white speck in my right eye which was to blind it and make me squint; but this was not yet apparent. Hundreds of photographs were taken of me and my mother touched them up with coloured pencils. In one, which has survived, I am fair and pink, with curls, my cheeks are plump and I am wearing a look of kindly deference to the established order; my mouth is swollen with arrogant hypocrisy: I know my worth.

It was not enough for me to be naturally good; I had to be a prophet: truth speaks through the mouths of children. Still close to nature, they are cousins of the wind and the sea: their babblings provide broad and vague instruction for anyone who can understand them. My grandfather had crossed the Lake of Geneva with Henri Bergson: 'I was wild with enthusiasm,' he used to say, 'I had not eyes enough to watch the glittering wave-crests, to follow the shimmering of the water. But Bergson sat on a suitcase, staring at his feet.' From that incident on a journey, he concluded that poetic meditation was preferable to philosophy. He meditated on me: sitting in a deckchair in the garden, a glass of beer within arm's reach, he used to watch me running and leaping, seeking wisdom in my confused words and finding it. Later on, I laughed at his foolishness; I am sorry that I did: it was the influence of death. Charles fought anxiety with ecstasy. He was admiring in me the world's fine handiwork so as to convince himself that everything was good, even our shabby ends. He was off in search of the same nature which was preparing to reclaim him, on mountain-tops, in the waves, among the stars and at the spring of my young life, so that he could embrace it whole and accept it all, including the pit that was being dug for him. It was not Truth but *his* death which spoke to him through my mouth. It is not surprising that the insipid happiness of my early years sometimes had a morbid flavour: I owed my freedom to a chance death and my importance to a long-awaited decease. So what? All Pythiases are dead, everyone knows that; all children are mirrors of death.

Then my grandfather enjoyed upsetting his sons. This awesome father had spent his life crushing them; now they came in on tiptoe and caught him at an infant's knees: it was enough to break their hearts! In the struggle between the generations, children and old people often join forces: the first deliver the oracles; the second decipher them. Nature speaks and experience translates: all adults have to do is shut up. If you have no children, a poodle will do: last year, at the dogs' cemetery, I recognized, in the quavering oration which ran on from tomb to tomb, my grandfather's maxims; dogs know how to love; they are more affectionate, more loyal than men; they have tact and an unfailing instinct which allows them to recognize Good and to tell good men from bad. 'Polonius,' said one grief-stricken woman, 'you are better than I: you would not have survived me; but I am surviving you.' I had an American friend with me: disgusted, he kicked a cement dog and broke its ear. He was right: when you love children and dogs *too much*, you love them instead of adults.

So I was a poodle of the future; I made prophecies. I said precocious things, and they were remembered and repeated to me: I learnt to make up others. I said grown-up things: I knew, effortlessly, how to say things 'in advance of my age'. These things were poems: the recipe was simple: you had to trust yourself to the Devil, haphazardly, in the void, borrow whole sentences from adults, put them together and keep saying them without understanding them. In short, I delivered genuine oracles and each person interpreted them to his own taste. Good was born in the depths of my heart and Truth in the youthful darkness of my Understanding. I admired myself on trust: it so happened that my words and gestures had a quality which escaped me yet which sprang to the eyes of grown-ups; never mind! I would unfailingly offer them the delicate pleasure refused me. My clowning took on the appearances of generosity: some poor people were desolate because they had no child; touched, I would tear myself from nothingness in a surge of altruism and put on the disguise of childhood to give them the illusion of having a son. My mother and grandmother often invited me to repeat the act of outstanding goodness which brought me into the world: they used to indulge Charles Schweitzer's little manias and his passion for melodramatic effects, and arrange surprises for him. I would be hidden behind a piece of furniture, I would hold my breath, the women would leave the room and pretend to forget me and I would vanish into thin air; my grandfather would come into the room, tired and depressed, just as he would have been had I not existed; suddenly, I would emerge from my hiding-place and do him the favour of being born. He would see me, and enter into the game: his face would change and he would fling his arms in the air; my presence transformed him. In a word, I gave myself; I gave myself all the time and everywhere; I, too, only had to push open a door to feel that I was making an appearance. I would pile my bricks on top of each other, shape my sand-castles and call out loud; someone would come and emit exclamations: I had made another person happy. Meals, sleep and precautions against bad weather were the major events and the major obligations of a life that was all ceremony.

22

I ate in public, like a king: if I ate *well*, I was congratulated; even my grandmother would exclaim: 'How clever of him to be hungry!'

I never stopped creating myself; I was both giver and gift. If my father had lived, I would have known my rights and duties; he died, so I did not: I had no rights because I was overwhelmed with love; I had no duties because I did everything through love. One mission only: to give pleasure; everything was for show. How our family wallowed in generosity: my grandfather kept me alive and I made him happy; my mother devoted herself to us all. Today, when I think about it, this devotion alone strikes me as genuine; but we tended to let it go without a word. No matter: our life was one long succession of ceremonies and we spent our time heaping ourselves with praise. I respected grown-ups provided they idolized me; I was as frank, open and gentle as a girl. I was pious and people trusted me: everyone was good because everyone was happy. I saw society as a strict hierarchy of merits and powers. Those at the top of the ladder gave all they had to those below them. Yet I took care not to place myself on the highest rung: I was not unaware that it was reserved for grave and well-intentioned figures who maintained order. I placed myself on a small marginal perch, not far away from them, and my radiance covered the ladder from head to foot. In short, I did all I could to stand aside from secular power: neither above nor below, but elsewhere. A cleric's grandson, I was a cleric from childhood; I had the unctuousness of the princes of the Church and the hearty manner of the priesthood. I treated inferiors as equals: this was a pious deceit which I practised on them to make them happy and which meant that they had, to some extent, been taken in. I spoke to my nurse, the postman and my dog in patient, even tones. In this ordered world there were poor people. There were also sheep with five legs, Siamese twins and railway accidents: these anomalies were no one's fault. The poor and virtuous did not know that their mission was to exercise our generosity; those who were poor and ashamed slunk along the walls; I would go over to them, slip a penny into their hands and, most important, make them

a present of a fine, democratic smile. I found that they looked
stupid and I did not like touching them, but I made myself: it
was a test; and then they must love me: that love would beau-
tify their lives. I knew they lacked the necessities of life and I
liked to give them more than they needed. Besides, however
wretched they were, they would never suffer as much as my
grandfather: when he was small, he used to rise before dawn
and get dressed in the dark; in the winter, he had to break the
ice in the water-jug to wash himself. Happily, things had sorted
themselves out since then: my grandfather believed in Progress
and so did I: Progress, that long and arduous road which led
to myself.

It was Paradise. Each morning, I woke in a daze of joy,
marvelling at the wild stroke of fortune by which I had been
born into the most united family in the most beautiful country
in the world. Malcontents shocked me: what had they to complain about? They were mutineers. My grandmother, in particular, caused me the greatest anxiety: it was painful to me to
realize that she did not admire me enough. In fact, Louise had
seen through me. She openly blamed in me the quackery for
which she had never dared to reproach her husband: I was a
buffoon, a clown, a sham, and she ordered me to stop my
monkey-tricks. I was so angry that I suspected her of making
fun of my grandfather too: it was the 'Spirit of constant denial'.
I *answered back* and she insisted on my begging her pardon;
confident of support, I refused. My grandfather leapt at the
opportunity of showing how weak she was: he took my side
against his wife who got up, beside herself, and went and shut
herself in her room. My mother, worried and afraid of the spite
of my grandmother, spoke quietly and, humbly, laid the
blame on her father who shrugged and retired to his study; in
the end, she begged me to go and ask for forgiveness. I rejoiced
in my power: I was St Michael and I had defeated the Evil One.
Finally, I went and perfunctorily said I was sorry. Apart from
this, of course, I adored her: *because* she was my grandmother.
It had been suggested that I should call her Mamie, and the
head of the family by his Alsatian first name, Karl. 'Karl et

24

Mamie' sounded better than Romeo and Juliet or Philemon and Baucis. My mother would say to me a hundred times a day, not without intent: 'Karlémami are waiting; Karlémami will be pleased, Karlémami . . .', suggesting by the intimacy of these four syllables complete harmony between the persons. I was only half taken in, but I contrived to appear entirely so: at least in my own eyes. The word shed its influence on the thing; through Karlémami, I could maintain the flawless unity of the family and transfer a fair share of Charles's merits to Louise's head. My grandmother, suspect and sinful, for ever on the verge of slipping, was restrained by the arm of an angel, through the power of a word.

There were some genuinely wicked people: the Prussians, who had taken away Alsace-Lorraine and all our clocks, except the black marble one which decorated my grandfather's mantelpiece, and which had in fact been presented to him by a group of German students; you wondered where they had stolen it. I was bought Hansi's books and shown the pictures in them: I felt no dislike for these big men in pink icing-sugar, who looked so much like my uncles from Alsace. My grandfather, who had opted for France in 1871, used to go, now and then, to Gunsbach and Pfaffenhofen, to visit those who had remained. I would accompany him. In the train, when a German ticket-inspector asked him for his ticket, or in cafés when a waiter was slow to take his order, Charles Schweitzer would go purple in the face with patriotic rage; the two women would cling to his arms: 'Charles! What are you dreaming of? They'll throw us out and then where will you be?' My grandfather would raise his voice: 'I would like to see them throw me out: this is my home!' They would push me towards him. I would gaze at him pleadingly and he would calm down: 'It's only because of the boy,' he would say with a sigh, running his dry fingers through my hair. These scenes turned me against him yet did not make me feel indignant towards those who had occupied the district. What was more, Charles never failed, at Gunsbach, to rail against his sister-in-law; several times a week, he would fling his napkin down on the table and leave the dining-room with a slam of the door: yet she was not German. After meals, we would go and weep and moan at his feet and he would respond with a haughty look. It was impossible not to agree with my grandmother's opinion: 'Alsace means nothing to him; he shouldn't go back there so often.' Besides, I was not all that fond of the Alsatians who treated me with lack of respect and I was not too annoyed that they had been taken away from us. Apparently, I used to go too often to the Pfaffenhofen grocer, Monsieur Blumenfeld, and worry him over some trifle. My aunt Caroline 'remarked on it' to my mother; it was passed on to me; for once, Louise and I were allies: she loathed her hus-' band's family. In Strasbourg, I heard, from an hotel bedroom, where we were all gathered, some thin, moony sounds and I rushed to the window: the army! I was delighted to see Prussia march by to the sound of this infantile music and clapped my hands. My grandfather remained on his chair, growling; my mother came and whispered to me to leave the window. I obeyed rather sulkily. I hated the Germans, by God, but only half-heartedly. Anyway, Charles could permit himself only a very slight touch of chauvinism: in 1911, we left Meudon to settle in Paris, at No. 1 rue le Goff; he had had to retire and had just founded, to support us, an Institute of Modern Languages: in it, French was taught to visiting foreigners. By the direct method. The majority of the pupils came from Germany. They paid well: my grandfather slipped their gold coins into his jacket pocket without ever counting them; my grandmother, who slept badly, used to sneak into the hall at night to collect her tithe 'on the sly', as she herself told her daughter: in short, the enemy was keeping us; a Franco-German war would have given us back Alsace and ruined the Institute; Charles was for preserving the Peace. And then there were some good Germans who used to come and lunch with us: a red-faced, hairy woman novelist whom Louise with a little jealous laugh used to call 'Charles's Dulcinea' and a bald doctor who used to push my mother against the doors and try to kiss her; when she made a timid complaint, my grandfather would explode: 'You're getting me in everyone's bad books!' Then he would shrug and conclude: 'You've been dreaming, my girl,' so that she was the one who felt guilty. All these guests realized that they had to go

26

into raptures over my merits, and they used to pat me obediently: in spite of their origins, they must have preserved some obscure notion of Good. On the anniversary of the foundation of the Institute, there were more than a hundred guests and light champagne, and my mother and Mademoiselle Moutet played Bach duets; in a blue muslin dress, with stars in my hair and wings, I went from one person to the next, offering them mandarin oranges from a basket, as they exclaimed: 'He *really* *is* an angel!' After all, they were not so bad. Of course, we had not given up the idea of avenging martyred Alsace; together, in whispers, like our cousins in Gunsbach and Pfaffenhofen, we killed the Boche by ridicule; we laughed a hundred times over, unwearyingly, at the girl-student who had just written in a French composition: '*Charlotte était percluse de douleurs sur la tombe de Werther*',* and at the young teacher who, in the course of a dinner, examined his slice of melon distrustfully and finally ate the lot, pips and rind included. These blunders inclined me to indulgence: the Germans were inferior beings who were lucky to be our neighbours; we would enlighten them.

A kiss without a moustache, they said then, is like an egg without salt; I will add to it: and it is like Good without Evil, like my life between 1905 and 1914. If a person can define himself only through opposition, I was the undefined made flesh and blood; if love and hate are the two sides of the same coin, I loved nothing and no one. It was a good thing: you cannot expect to hate and please at the same time. Nor to please and love.

Was I a Narcissus then? Not even that: too anxious to win others, I forgot myself. After all, it gave me little pleasure to make mud-pies or scribble, my natural needs: for them to have value in my eyes, at least one grown-up had to rhapsodize over my works. Fortunately, there was no lack of applause: whether they were listening to my gibberish or the Art of Fugue, adults wore the same smile of conspiratorial and mischievous relish. This shows what I really was: a cultural possession. I was impregnated with culture and I returned it to the family

* Charlotte was crippled with sorrows (pains) on Werther's tomb.

27

like a radiance, as pools in the evening give back the heat of the day.

I began my life as I shall no doubt end it: among books. In my grandfather's study, they were everywhere; it was forbidden to dust them except once a year, before the October term. Even before I could read, I already revered these raised stones; upright or leaning, wedged together like bricks on the library shelves or nobly spaced like avenues of dolmens, I felt that our family prosperity depended on them. They were all alike, and I was romping about in a tiny sanctuary, surrounded by squat, ancient monuments which had witnessed my birth, which would witness my death and whose permanence guaranteed me a future as calm as my past. I used to touch them in secret to honour my hands with their dust but I did not have much idea what to do with them and each day I was present at ceremonies whose meaning escaped me: my grandfather – so clumsy, normally, that my grandmother buttoned his gloves for him – handled these cultural objects with the dexterity of an officiating priest. Hundreds of times I saw him get up absent-mindedly, walk round the table, cross the room in two strides, unhesitatingly pick out a volume without allowing himself time for choice, run through it as he went back to his armchair, with a combined movement of his thumb and right forefinger, and, almost before he sat down, open it with a flick 'at the right page', making it creak like a shoe. I sometimes got close enough to observe these boxes which opened like oysters and I discovered the nakedness of their internal organs, pale, dank, slightly blistered pages, covered with small black veins, which drank ink and smelt of mildew.

In my grandmother's room, the books were lying down; she used to borrow them from a lending-library and I never saw more than two at a time. These trashy works reminded me of New Year sweetmeats because their shiny flexible covers seemed to be cut out of glazed paper. Bright, white, almost new, they served as an excuse for petty mysteries. Each Friday, my grandmother would get dressed to go out and say: 'I'm going to take *them* back'; when she returned, and had taken off her black hat and her veil, she would take *them* out of her muff and I would wonder, mystified: 'Are they the same ones?' She used to 'cover' them carefully and then, having chosen one, she would settle herself by the window, in her winged armchair, put on her spectacles, sigh with pleasure and weariness, and lower her eyelids with a delicately voluptuous smile which I have since discovered on the lips of the Mona Lisa; my mother would fall silent, inviting me to keep quiet, and I would think about Mass, death or sleep: I invested myself with a holy silence. From time to time, Louise would give a chuckle; she would call to her daughter, point at a line and the two women would exchange a conspiratorial look. Yet I did not care for these over-elegant works; they were intruders and my grandfather did not hide the fact that they were part of an exclusively feminine, inferior cult: on Sundays, he would go, for want of anything better to do, into my grandmother's room and would plant himself in front of her without finding anything to say: everyone would look at him, he would drum on the window-pane and then, void of ideas, he would turn back to Louise and snatch her book away from her: 'Charles!' she would cry out angrily, 'you'll lose my page!' Eyebrows raised, he would already be reading; suddenly his forefinger would rap the book: 'Don't understand!' 'But why do you want to understand?' my grandmother would say: 'You read between the lines!' In the end, he would fling the book down on tne table and go out shrugging his shoulders.

He was obviously right because he was in the profession. I knew that: he had shown me, on a shelf of the library, some strong, stiff-backed volumes, bound in brown cloth. 'Your grandfather wrote those, my boy.' What pride! I was the grandson of a craftsman who specialized in the manufacture of holy objects, as worthy as an organ-builder or an ecclesiastical tailor. I saw him at work: each year, the *Deutsches Lesebuch* was reissued. During the holidays, the entire family waited impatiently for the proofs: Charles could not stand inactivity so, to pass the time, he used to get cross. The postman would at last bring the large, flabby parcels and the string would be cut with scissors; my grandfather would undo the galley-proofs, spread them on the dining-room table and slash them with red lines; he would swear between his teeth, calling on the name of the Lord at every printing error, but he would not shout except when the maid wanted to lay the table. Everyone would be happy. Standing on a chair, I would gaze in ecstasies at the black lines, scored with blood. Charles Schweitzer told me that he had a mortal enemy, his Publisher. My grandfather had never learned to count: prodigal out of carelessness, generous out of show, he eventually succumbed, much later, to that octogenarian disease, avarice, the result of impotence and the fear of death. At that time, it showed itself only in an odd suspiciousness: when he received a cheque for the amount of his royalties, he would raise his arms to the sky and cry out that they were slitting his throat or else he would go in to my grandmother and announce gloomily: 'My publisher's robbing me under my very eyes.' Astonished, I learned about man's exploitation of man. Yet, without this abomination, fortunately limited, the world would have been perfect: the employers gave what they could and the workers got what they deserved. Why did those vampires of publishers have to spoil it all by sucking my poor grandfather's blood? My respect grew for this holy man whose devotion found no reward: I was prepared in good time to see teaching as a priesthood and literature as a passion.

I was still unable to read but I was snobbish enough to insist on having *my* books. My grandfather went along to his scoundrel of a publisher and was given *Les Contes* by Maurice Bouchor, the poet, tales drawn from folklore and adapted to children's tastes by a man who, so they said, still had the eyes of a child. I wanted to begin my appropriation ceremonies on the spot. I took the two small volumes, sniffed at them, felt them, opened them casually 'at the right page' and made them creak. It was no good: I did not feel that I owned them. I tried without greater success to treat them as dolls, cradle them, kiss them and beat them. On the verge of tears, I finally laid them on my mother's lap. She looked up from her work: 'What do you want me to read, darling? About the Fairies?' I asked incredulously: 'Are there Fairies *in there*?' I knew the tale well:

my mother often told it to me while she was washing my face, breaking off to massage me with eau-de-Cologne or to pick up, from under the bath, the soap which had slipped from her hands, and I would listen with half an ear to an all-too-familiar story; all I wanted to see was Anne-Marie, the young girl of my mornings; all I wanted to hear was her voice, disturbed by servitude; I loved her half-completed sentences, her always slow-to-come words and her brusque confidence, quickly defeated and put to rout, which disappeared with a pleasant fraying sound, and then re-established itself after a silence. The story was secondary: it was the link between her soliloquies. All the while she was talking, we were alone and private, far from man, gods and priests, two does in the wood, with those other does, the Fairies; I never could believe that a whole book could have been written to feature this episode in our profane life, which smelt of soap and eau-de-Cologne.

Anne-Marie made me sit down in front of her, on my little chair; she leant over, lowered her eyelids and went to sleep. From this mask-like face issued a plaster voice. I grew bewildered: who was talking? about what? and to whom? My mother had disappeared: not a smile or trace of complicity. I was an exile. And then I did not recognize the language. Where did she get her confidence? After a moment, I realized: it was the book that was talking. Sentences emerged that frightened me: they were like real centipedes; they swarmed with syllables and letters, span out their diphthongs and made their double consonants hum; fluting, nasal, broken up with sighs and pauses, rich in unknown words, they were in love with themselves and their meanderings and had no time for me: sometimes they disappeared before I could understand them; at others, I had understood in advance and they went rolling on nobly towards their end without sparing me a comma. These words were obviously not meant for me. The tale itself was in its Sunday best: the woodcutter, the woodcutter's wife and their daughters, the fairy, all those little people, our fellow-creatures, had acquired majesty; their rags were magnificently described, words left their mark on objects, transforming actions into rituals and events into ceremonies. Someone began to ask

31

questions: my grandfather's publisher, who specialized in putting out school editions, lost no opportunity of exercising the intelligence of his young readers. It was as if a child were being quizzed: what would he have done in the woodcutter's place? Which of the two sisters did he prefer? Why? Did he agree with Babette's punishment? But this child was not entirely me and I was afraid to reply. I did reply, though; my feeble voice grew faint and I felt I was turning into someone else. Anne-Marie, too, with her blind soothsayer's look, was someone else: it was as if I were every mother's child and she were every child's mother. When she stopped reading, I quickly took back the books and carried them off under my arm without a word of thanks.

In the long run, I came to enjoy this release which tore me out of myself: Maurice Bouchor leaned over my childhood with that universal concern which heads of departments have for customers in big stores; that flattered me. I came to prefer prefabricated tales to improvised ones; I became sensitive to the unchanging sequence of words: they would return each time you read them, always the same ones and always in the same order, and I would wait for them. In Anne-Marie's stories, the characters lived haphazardly, as she herself did: they acquired fates. I was at Mass: I was present at the endless re-iteration of names and events.

Then I became jealous of my mother and I decided to usurp her role. I seized upon a work called *Tribulations d'un Chinois en Chine* and took it away to a box-room; there, perched on a folding bedstead, I pretended to read: my eyes followed the black lines without skipping a single one and I told myself a story out loud, taking care to pronounce every syllable. I was discovered – or I let myself be discovered; there were cries of admiration and it was decided that it was time I was taught the alphabet. I was zealous as a catechumen; I even gave myself private lessons: I climbed on to my folding bedstead with Hector Malot's *Sans famille*, which I knew by heart, and, half-reciting, half-deciphering it, I went through every page, one after another: when the last was turned, I knew how to read.

I was wild with delight: those withered voices in their little nature-books, those voices which my grandfather revived with a glance, which he heard and which I did not hear, were mine! I would listen to them, I would fill myself with ceremonious speeches and I would know everything. I was allowed to wander about in the library and I mounted an offensive on human knowledge. That was what made me. Later on, I was to hear anti-Semites reproach the Jews a hundred times over for being ignorant of nature's lessons and mysteries. I used to reply: 'In that case I'm more Jewish than they.' I would search vainly in myself for the overloaded memories and sweet unreason of rustic childhoods. I never scratched the soil or searched for nests; I never looked for plants or threw stones at birds. But books were my birds and my nests, my pets, my stable and my countryside; the library was the world trapped in a mirror; it had its infinite breadth, its variety and its unpredictability. I set off on incredible adventures: this meant climbing on chairs and tables, at the risk of provoking avalanches which might have buried me. For a long while, the works on the top shelf remained out of my reach; others, almost as soon as I found them, were snatched from my hands; still others were hidden: 1 had taken them, started to read them and thought I had returned them to their places; it took a week to find them again. I met with some horrible encounters: I would open an album and come on a coloured illustration; hideous insects would swarm before my very eyes. Lying on the carpet, I undertook barren journeys through Fontenelle, Aristophanes and Rabelais: the sentences resisted me in the same way as objects; I had to watch them, go round them, pretend to move away and then suddenly come back at them to catch them off their guard: most of the time, they preserved their secrets. I was La Pérouse, Magellan and Vasco da Gama; I discovered strange natives: *'Heautontimorouménos'* in a translation of Terence into alexandrines and *'idiosyncrasie'* in a work on comparative literature. *Apocope, Chiasme, Parangon* and a hundred other obscure and distant Kaffirs rose up at the turn of a page and their mere appearance threw out the entire paragraph. I did not learn the meanings of these hard, black words until ten or fifteen years later and, even today, they still remain opaque: they are the leaf-mould of my memory.

The library contained little besides the French and German classics. There were some grammars, too, a few famous novels, a selection of Maupassant's *Contes choisis*, some art books – a *Rubens*, a *Van Dyck*, a *Dürer*, and a *Rembrandt* – which my grandfather's pupils had presented to him some New Year. A small world. But the *Grand Larousse* took the place of everything: I would pick a volume at random, from behind the desk, on the last but one shelf, A-Bello, Belloc-Ch or Ci-D, Mele-Po or Pr-Z (these associations of syllables had become proper names indicating areas of human knowledge: there was the Ci-D region and the Pr-Z region, with their fauna and flora, their towns, their great men and their battles); I would lay them down with difficulty on my grandfather's blotter, open them, and I would go nesting after real birds and chasing after real butterflies perched on real flowers. Men and beasts were there, *in person*: the illustrations were their bodies and the text their souls, their particular essences; outside the walls, you met vague shapes which more or less resembled the archetypes without attaining to their perfection: in the Zoo, the monkeys were less like monkeys and, in the Luxembourg Gardens, men were less like men. A Platonist by condition, I moved from knowledge to its object; I found ideas more real than things, because they were the first to give themselves to me and because they gave themselves like things. I met the universe in books: assimilated, classified, labelled and studied, but still impressive; and I confused the chaos of my experiences through books with the hazardous course of real events. Hence my idealism which it took me thirty years to undo.

Everyday life was crystal-clear: we used to meet well-balanced people who spoke up loud and clear, based their convictions on healthy principles, on the Wisdom of Nations, and deigned to single themselves out from ordinary persons only by a certain affectedness of the soul to which I was entirely used. Their opinions, no sooner voiced, convinced me by their crystalline, artless truth; if they wanted to justify their actions, they put forward such boring reasons that they could not help

34

but be true; their moral dilemmas, willingly expounded, worried me less than they edified me: they were artificial conflicts resolved in advance and always the same ones; their faults, when they recognized them, carried little weight: their haste and their reasonable but no doubt exaggerated ill-temper had impaired their judgements; fortunately, they had realized it in time; the faults of the absent, more serious, were never unforgivable: at home, we never ran people down; we recognized, in sorrow, defects of character. I used to listen, understand and approve; I found these statements reassuring and I was not mistaken because they were meant to reassure: there was nothing that could not be remedied and, deep down, nothing stirred and the vain movements of the surface could not hide from us the calm death house that is our lot.

When our visitors had said good-bye, I would be left alone; I would escape from this boring cemetery and I would go and rejoin life and frivolity in books. All I had to do was open one to rediscover in it those anxious, inhuman thoughts whose pomps and shadows passed my understanding, which leapt from one idea to another, so quickly that I slackened my grip, a hundred times a page, and, lost and bewildered, let them go. I witnessed events which my grandfather would unquestionably have deemed improbable and yet which had the resounding truth of the written word. Characters would rise up without a word of warning, fall in love, quarrel and murder each other; the survivor would be racked with grief and rejoin in the tomb the friend or the mistress he had just murdered. What was I to do? Was I expected, like the grown-ups, to blame, congratulate and forgive? But these individuals did not seem to govern themselves by our principles, and their motives, even when supplied, eluded me. Brutus killed his son and so did Mateo Falcone.* Therefore the practice seemed fairly common. Yet no one around me had had recourse to it. In Meudon, my grandfather had quarrelled with my uncle Émile and I had heard them shouting in the garden: but it did not seem to me that he had thought of killing him. How did he judge fathers who killed their children? I kept aloof: my life was not in danger

* The main character in a short story of the same name by Mérimée.

because I was an orphan and these ritual killings mildly amused me, but, in the stories made about them, I sensed an approval which baffled me. I had to force myself not to spit on the illustration which showed Horace, with helmet and naked sword, chasing after poor Camille. Karl sometimes used to hum:

> *On n' peut pas êt' plus proch' parents*
> *Que frère et soeur assurément.* . . . *

This worried me: if, by chance, I had been given a sister, would she have been closer to me than Anne-Marie? Or than Karlémami? Then she would have been my mistress. Mistress was still only a shadowy word which I often came across in Corneille's tragedies. Lovers kissed and promised to sleep in the same bed (a strange custom: why not in twin beds as my mother and I did?). I knew nothing more but, beneath the glossy surface of the idea, I sensed a hairy body. In any case, as a brother, I would have been incestuous. I used to dream about it. Origin? A cover-up for forbidden emotions? It may well be. I had an older sister, my mother, and I wanted a younger one. Even today – 1963 – it is the only family relationship which appeals to me.† I made the serious mistake of often looking among women for this sister who had never turned up: appeal rejected, ordered to pay costs. Even so, writing these lines, I feel again the anger I felt towards Camille's murderer; it is so fresh and so alive that I wonder if Horace's crime is not one of the sources of my anti-militarism: soldiers kill their sisters. I would have shown him, the old ruffian. Down with him, for a

* 'There's certainly no closer tie than that between brother and sister.'
† When I was about ten I used to adore reading *Les Transatlantiques*: in it were a little American and his sister, very innocent, by the way. But I identified myself with the boy and, through him, I loved Biddy, the little girl. For a long time, I have dreamed of writing a short story about two lost and quietly incestuous children. Echoes of this fantasy can be found in my writings: Orestes and Electra in *Les Mouches*, Boris and Ivich in *Les Chemins de la liberté*, Frantz and Leni in *Les Séquestrés d'Altona*. Only the last couple do anything about it. What attracted me in this family link was not so much the temptation to love as the prohibition against making love; I liked incest, with its mixture of fire and ice, enjoyment and frustration, so long as it remained platonic. (*Author's footnote.*)

start! And a dozen bullets in his guts. I would turn the pages; some printed words would show me my mistake: the sorori- cide had to be *acquitted*. For a few moments, I would snort and stamp my foot, like a decoyed bull. And then I would quickly stifle my rage. That was how it was; I must make the best of it: I was too young. I had got it all wrong; the need for this acquittal was rightly established by the numerous alexandrines which remained obstinately closed to me or which I had impatiently skipped. I used to love this uncertainty and the way the story evaded me on all sides: that put me on the wrong scent. I read the concluding pages of *Madame Bovary* twenty times; in the end, I knew whole paragraphs by heart and still the poor widower's actions did not seem any clearer; he found some letters: was that any reason for letting his beard grow? He glanced at Rodolphe darkly, because he felt bitter towards him – but *what for*? And why did he say to him: 'I don't bear you any grudge'? Why did Rodolphe find him 'comic and rather despicable'? Afterwards, Charles Bovary died: of grief? of an illness? And why did the doctor open him up when it was all over? I used to enjoy this stubborn, unending resistance; mystified and exhausted, I relished the equivocal pleasure of understanding and yet not understanding: this was the com- plexity of the world; I found the human heart, which my grand- father discussed freely at home, empty and insipid everywhere except in books. Intoxicating names played on my moods, plunging me into inexplicable terror or melancholy. I used to say 'Charbovary' and see, out of nowhere, a tall bearded man in rags walking about a yard: it was unbearable. At the source of these agonizing pleasures was a combination of two contra- dictory fears. I was afraid of plunging head first into a mythical universe and wandering about in it for ever, in the company of Horace and Charbovary, with no hope of seeing the rue le Goff, Karlémami and my mother again. And, on the other hand, I sensed that these processions of words presented to adult readers significances which escaped me. Through my eyes, I drew into my head poisoned words, infinitely richer than I knew; a strange force reconstructed in me, through speech, stories of angry men who did not concern me, a dreadful grief or the wreck of a life: would I not be infected and die of poisoning? Absorbing the Word and absorbed by the image, I escaped, in the end, only through the incompatibility of these two simultaneous perils. At dusk, lost in a jungle of words, trembling at the least sound, mistaking the creak of the parquet floor for exclamations, I thought I was discovering language in its raw state, without man. With what cowardly relief, what disappointment, I returned to the boredom of family life when my mother came in, put on the light and said: 'My poor darling, you're ruining your eyes!' My face drawn, I would leap to my feet, shout, rush and clown about. But even in my re-won childhood, I would worry: *what* were the books talking about? Who wrote them? Why? I confided these anxieties to my grandfather who, on reflection, decided that it was time to liberate me and did it so effectively that it left its mark on me.

For a long time, he had been in the habit of jogging me up and down on his outstretched leg singing: '*A cheval sur mon bidet*; *quand il trotte il fait des pets*', and I would snigger. He stopped singing: he sat me on his knee and looked me in the eyes: 'I am man,' he kept saying in an official voice, 'I am man, and nothing human is foreign to me.' He used to exaggerate a lot: as Plato expelled poets, so Karl drove engineers, merchants and probably officers from his Republic. Factories ruined the countryside; of the pure sciences, he enjoyed only the purity. My uncle Georges would take us to visit the foundries in Guérigny, where we used to spend the second half of July: it was hot, and rough, ill-dressed men would jostle us; deafened by the immense noise, I used to die of fear and boredom; my grandfather would whistle as he watched the flow of metal, out of politeness, but his eyes remained dead. In Auvergne, on the other hand, in August, he used to ferret about among the villages, stop in front of old buildings and tap the brickwork with the end of his walking-stick: 'What you see there, my child,' he would say brightly, 'is a Romano-Gallic wall.' He also appreciated church architecture and, although he loathed papists, he never missed going into churches if they were Gothic; if Romanesque, it depended on his mood. He hardly ever went to concerts now, but he had been to them: he liked Beethoven for his pomp and his large orchestras; Bach, too, but without enthusiasm. Sometimes, he would go over to the piano and, without sitting down, would strike a few chords with his stiff fingers: my grandmother would say, with a tight smile: 'Charles is composing.' Her sons – especially Georges – had become good performers who hated Beethoven and preferred chamber music to all else; these differences of taste did not worry my grandfather; he would say amiably: 'The Schweitzers are born musicians.' Because at a week old I seemed to cheer up at the clink of a spoon, he had decreed that I had an ear.

Stained-glass windows, flying buttresses, sculptured portals, crucifixions carved in wood or stone, Meditations in verse or poetic Harmonies: such Humanities led us straight to the Divine. The more so, because natural beauty had to be added to them. One and the same breath shaped God's works and great human works; one and the same rainbow shone in the spray of waterfalls, sparkled between the lines of Flaubert, and gleamed in Rembrandt's chiaroscuro: it was the Spirit. The Spirit spoke to God about Men and it bore witness of God to men. In Beauty, my grandfather saw the presence of Truth made flesh and the source of the loftiest aspirations. In certain exceptional circumstances – when a storm broke in the mountains or when Victor Hugo was inspired – it was possible to attain to the Sublime Point where Truth, Beauty and Goodness became one.

I had found my religion: nothing seemed more important to me than a book. I saw the library as a temple. Grandson of a 'priest', I lived on the roof of the world, on the sixth floor, perched on the highest branch of the Central Tree: its trunk was the lift-shaft. I came and went on the balcony, cast a glance from on high at the passers-by, waved through the railings at Lucette Moreau, my neighbour, who was my age and had the same fair curls and youthful femininity, and retired into my *cella* or *pronaos*, but never went down *in person*: when my mother took me to the Luxembourg Gardens – that is to say, every day – I lent my human body to these lowly regions but my glorious substance never left its perch, and I believe it is still

39

there. Every man has his natural place; it is not pride or worth that settles its height: childhood decides everything. Mine is a sixth floor in Paris with a view of the rooftops. For a long time, I suffocated in valleys and plains overwhelmed me: I dragged myself round the planet Mars and the pressure crushed me; all I had to do to be happy again was climb on to a molehill: I was back on my symbolic sixth floor and once again breathing the rarefied air of Belles-Lettres. The Universe lay spread at my feet and each thing was humbly begging for a name, and giving it one was like both creating it and taking it. Without this fundamental illusion, I should never have written.

Today, 22 April 1963, I am correcting this manuscript on the tenth floor of a new house: through the open window, I can see a cemetery, Paris and the blue hills of Saint-Cloud. This shows my pertinacity. Yet everything has changed. If, as a child, I had wished to deserve this exalted position, my love of pigeon-lofts would seem to have indicated some play of ambition or vanity or compensation for my lack of height. But no; it was not a question of climbing my sacred tree: I was there and I refused to come down; it was not that I wished to set myself up above men: I wanted to live in pure ether among the airy likenesses of Things. Later on, far from clinging to balloons, I made every effort to sink down: I had to put lead soles on my shoes. With luck, on bare sands I sometimes managed to brush against underwater species, whose names I had to invent. At other times, I was powerless: an irresistible lightness buoyed me up. In the end, my altimeter went out of order: sometimes I am a Cartesian diver, sometimes a deep sea diver, often both at the same time, as it should be in our profession: I dwell in the air by habit and I nose about down below without too much hope.

Yet I had to be told about authors. My grandfather did so with discretion but without warmth. He taught me the names of famous men; when I was alone, I used to recite the list to myself, from Hesiod to Hugo, without a mistake: they were the Saints and the Prophets. Charles Schweitzer worshipped them, so he said. Yet they disturbed him: their unwelcome presence prevented him from attributing the works of Man directly to the Holy Ghost. He also cherished a secret preference for the anonymous, for builders who had had the modesty not to obtrude on their cathedrals, and for the innumerable authors of popular songs. He did not hate Shakespeare, whose identity was not established. Or Homer, for the same reason. Or several others whose existence was by no means certain. For those who had neither wished nor been able to wipe out the traces of their life, he found excuses provided they were dead. But he condemned his contemporaries wholesale, except for Anatole France and Courteline* who made him feel happy. Charles Schweitzer took a proud delight in the consideration shown to his great age, his culture, his looks and his virtues, and this disciple of Luther found nothing wrong in thinking, in true biblical fashion, that the Eternal had blessed his House. At table, he sometimes collected his thoughts sufficiently to take an off-hand view of his life, and would conclude: 'My children, how good it is to have nothing with which to reproach oneself.' His fits of anger, his majesty, his pride, his taste for the sublime concealed a timidity of spirit which sprang from his religion, his century, and his environment, the University. For this reason, he felt a secret disgust for the sacred monsters of his library, out-and-out blackguards whose books he regarded, in his heart of hearts, as absurdities. I was mistaken: I took the reserve which appeared beneath his forced enthusiasm for the severity of a judge; his 'priesthood' raised him above them. In any event, so the minister of the cult whispered to me, genius is merely a loan: it has to be earned through great suffering, through modestly yet staunchly endured trials; in the end you hear voices and write at their dictation. Between the first Russian revolution and the first world war, fifteen years after the death of Mallarmé, at the time when Daniel de Fontanin discovered *Les Nourritures terrestres*, a nineteenth-century man was imposing on his grandson ideas current under Louis-Philippe. This is how, they say, peasant customs can be explained: the fathers went off to the fields, leaving the sons in the care of the grandparents. I started off with an eighty-year

* Georges Courteline (pseudonym of Georges Moinaux, 1858–1929), author of light comedies.

41

handicap. Should I complain? I do not know: in our fluctuating societies, delays sometimes give you a start. Be that as it may, I was flung this bone to chew and I did it so effectively that I can see the light through it. My grandfather had hoped slyly to disgust me with writers, those go-betweens. He achieved the opposite result: I confused talent with merit. These honest men were like myself: when I was very good or when I endured my boils manfully, I had the right to a few laurels, to some reward; that was childhood. Karl Schweitzer showed me other children, watched over, put to the test, and rewarded like myself, who had managed to remain my age all their lives. Having neither brother nor sister nor any companions, I made them my first friends. They had loved, suffered harshly, like the heroes of their novels and, most important, they had ended up all right; I conjured up their torments with a rather cheerful sympathy: how happy these lads must have been when they were really miserable; they said to themselves: 'What a bit of luck! A good line will be born!'

In my eyes, they were not dead: at least, not quite; they were transformed into books. Corneille was a fat man with a gnarled red face and a leather back, who smelt of glue. This stern, difficult character, full of hard words, had corners which bruised my thighs when I carried him. But as soon as he was open, he presented me with his illustrations, soft and dark as secrets. Flaubert was a small, cloth bound, odourless, creature, dotted with freckles. Victor Hugo, the multifarious, nested on every shelf at the same time. So much for the bodies; the souls haunted the works: the pages were windows, there was a face pressed against the glass from outside, someone was watching me; I pretended not to notice anything and went on reading, my eyes riveted to the words, beneath the steady gaze of the late Chateaubriand. These anxieties did not last; the rest of the time, I adored my playmates. I set them above all else and I learnt without surprise that the Emperor Charles V had picked up Titian's paint-brush: good for him! – that was what a prince was for. Yet I did not respect them: why should I praise them for being great? They were only doing their duty. I blamed the others for being inferior. In short, I had got every-

42

thing upside down and I was making the rule of the exception: the human race became a select committee surrounded by friendly beasts. Above all, my grandfather treated them too badly for me to be able to take them entirely seriously. He had stopped reading after Victor Hugo's death; when he had nothing else to do, he re-read. But his business was translation. In his heart of hearts, the author of the *Deutsches Lesebuch* regarded world literature as his raw material. He classified authors artificially in order of merit, but this superficial hierarchy barely concealed his preferences, which were utilitarian: Maupassant made the best unseens for German students; Goethe, beating Gottfried Keller by a head, was unequalled for compositions. As a humanist, my grandfather thought little of novels; as a teacher, he valued them greatly because of their vocabulary. In the end, he could tolerate only selected passages and I saw him, a few years later, delighting in an extract from *Madame Bovary*, selected by Mironneau for his *Lectures*, while to Flaubert in full he had paid no attention for twenty years. I felt that he lived off these dead men, which did not simplify my relations with them: under pretext of worshipping them, he kept them in bonds and he did not scruple to carve them into slices to transpose them the more easily from one language to another. I discovered their greatness and wretchedness simultaneously. Mérimée had the misfortune to suit the Middle Form; consequently, he led a double life: on the fourth tier of the library, *Colomba* was an untouched dove with a hundred wings, frozen, offering herself and systematically ignored; no glance ever ravished her. But on the bottom shelf, this same virgin was imprisoned in a small, grubby, brown, smelly book; neither the story nor the language had changed, but there were notes in German and a vocabulary; I learned besides, a scandal unmatched since the rape of Alsace-Lorraine, that it had been published in Berlin. My grandfather put this book into his brief-case twice a week; he had covered it in stains, red marks and burns, and I loathed it: it was Mérimée humiliated. I had merely to open it to die of boredom: each syllable fell beneath my gaze separately as they did, at the Institute, from my grandfather's mouth. Printed in Germany to be read by Germans, what, anyway, were these known yet unrecognizable signs but counterfeits of French words? Yet another spy case: all you had to do was scratch them to discover, beneath their Gallic disguise, German words on the watch. I came to wonder if there were not two Colombas, one shy and true, the other false and didactic, just as there are two Yseults.

The trials of my young companions convinced me that I was their equal. I had neither their gifts nor their merits and I had not yet considered writing but, as the grandson of a priest, I was superior to them in birth: I was unquestionably dedicated: not to their always rather shocking martyrdoms but to some priesthood; I would be a guardian of culture, like Charles Schweitzer. And then I was alive and very active: I still did not know how to cut up the dead but I imposed my whims on them: I took them in my arms, carried them, laid them on the parquet floor, opened them, closed them again, and dragged them from nothingness only to plunge them back into it: these men-dummies were my dolls and I felt sorry for their wretched, paralysed state of survival called immortality.. My grandfather encouraged these familiarities: all children were inspired and had no reason to envy poets who themselves were quite simply children. I doted on Courteline and I would chase the cook into the kitchen to read aloud to her *Théodore cherche des allumettes*. My infatuation was thought amusing; care and attention enhanced it and made it into an avowed passion. One fine day my grandfather said to me casually: 'Courteline must be a good fellow. If you like him so much, why don't you write to him?' I wrote; Charles Schweitzer guided my hand and decided to leave a few spelling mistakes in my letter. Some newspapers reproduced it, a few years ago, and I read it with a certain annoyance. I ended with the words 'your friend-to-be', which seemed quite natural to me: Voltaire and Corneille were my familiars; how could a *living* writer refuse my friendship? Courteline refused it and did right: by replying to the grandchild, he would have got involved with the grandfather. At the time, we judged his silence severely. 'I grant', said Charles, 'he has a lot of work; but even so, you do answer a child.'

Even today, this minor vice of familiarity is still with me. I treat these famous dead like old school-friends; I talk bluntly about Baudelaire and Flaubert and, when I am reproached, I always feel like replying: 'Mind your own business. Your geniuses have belonged to me, I have held them in my hands, loved them passionately and with deep irreverence. Am I to wear kid gloves with them?' But I got rid of Karl's humanism, that prelate's humanism, the day I realized that every man is all men. How sad it is to be cured: language loses its magic; the heroes of the pen, once my equals, stripped of their privileges, have returned to the ranks: I wear mourning for them twice over.

What I have just written is false. True. Neither true nor false, like all that is written about madmen or about men. I have set down the facts as accurately as memory permits. But how far did I believe in my frenzy? That is the basic question and I cannot make up my mind about it. I realized afterwards that it is possible to know everything about our affections except their strength; that is to say, their sincerity. Actions themselves will not serve as a standard unless it has been proved that they are not gestures, which is not always easy. For instance, alone in the company of adults, I was an adult in miniature, and I read adult books; that already rings false because, at the same time, I remained a child. I am not making out that I was guilty: that is how it was, that is all; even so my explorations and searches did form part of the family Comedy and gave delight of which I was aware; yes, I was aware of it; every day, a wonder child reawakened the magic books which his grandfather had ceased to read. I lived beyond my age as people live beyond their means: enthusiastically, exhaustedly, expensively, and all for show. Almost before I had pushed open the library door, I was in the belly of a lazy old man: the large desk, the blotting-pad, the red and black ink-stains on the pink blotting-paper, the ruler, the glue-pot, the stale smell of tobacco and, in winter, the red glow of the Salamander stove, the cracking of the mica, all this was Karl personified, reified: it was all I needed to enter into a state of grace, so I ran to the books. Was I sincere? What does that mean? How could I pinpoint – especially after so many years – the intangible, shifting frontier that divides possession from play-acting? I used to lie on my stomach, facing the windows, a book open in front of me, a glass of water with a dash of wine to my right and a jam sandwich on a plate to my left. Even when alone, I was performing: Anne-Marie and Karlémami had turned these pages long before I was born – it was their knowledge which was displayed before my eyes. In the evening I was asked: 'What have you read? What did you make of it?' I was expecting this, I was in labour and I gave birth to a precocious remark; getting away from grown-ups in reading was the best way of communicating with them; when they were not there, their future gaze came in through the back of my head, came out again through my pupils and shot, at floor-level, along those oft-read sentences which I was reading for the first time. Seen, I saw myself: I saw myself reading as one hears oneself speak. Had I changed so much since the time when I pretended to decipher *Le Chinois en Chine* before I knew the alphabet? No: the game was continuing. The door would open behind me and someone had come to see 'what I was up to': I would cheat, leap to my feet, put Musset back in his place and immediately go on tiptoe, arms raised to take down the heavy Corneille; my enthusiasm could be gauged from my efforts and, behind me, I could hear an impressed voice whisper: 'He must *like* Corneille!' I did not like him: alexandrines repelled me. Luckily, the publisher had published only the best-known tragedies *in extenso*; he gave the titles and plots of the others: these were what interested me: 'Rodelinde, wife of Pertharite, king of the Lombards and conquered by Grimoald, is urged by Unulphe to give her hand to the foreign prince. . . .' I knew Rodogune, Théodore and Agésilas before Le Cid, before Cinna; I filled my mouth with sonorous names, my heart with sublime emotions and I took pains not to confuse the family relationships. They also said: 'The child's eager to learn; he devours *Larousse*!' and I let them say it. But I was not really learning: I had discovered that the encyclopedia contained summaries of plays and novels; I delighted in them.

I liked to please and I wanted to steep myself in culture: each day I recharged myself with holiness. Casually, sometimes: it was enough to lie down flat and turn the pages; often the works of my little friends served as my prayer-wheels. At the same time, I experienced joy and terror *in real earnest*; I sometimes used to forget my part and rush off at breakneck speed, borne away by a mad whale which was nothing less than the world. Make what you will of it! In any case, my eyes worked on the words: I had to test them, to decide on their meaning: in the long run, the Comedy of Culture cultivated me.

Yet I did some *genuine* reading: away from the sanctuary, in our bedroom or under the dining-room table; I did not discuss this with anyone, and no one, except my mother, discussed it with me. Anne-Marie had taken my fake fits of rage seriously. She confided her anxieties to Mamie. My grandmother was a sure ally: 'Charles goes too far,' she said. 'He's forcing the boy, I've seen him do it. We shall be in a fine state when the child's squeezed dry.' The two women also conjured up over-work and meningitis. It would have been dangerous and futile to make a frontal assault on my grandfather: so they came in on his flank. During one of our walks, Anne-Marie stopped, as if by chance, in front of the kiosk which still stands at the corner of the boulevard Saint-Michel and the rue Soufflot: I saw some marvellous pictures and their garish colours fascinated me; I wanted them and I got them; the trick had worked: each week I wanted *Cri-Cri*, *L'Épatant*, *Les Vacances*, Jean de la Hire's *Les Trois boy-scouts* and Arnould Galopin's *Le Tour du monde en aéroplane* which appeared in weekly parts on Thursdays. From one Thursday to the next, I used to think about the Eagles of the Andes, Marcel Dunot, the iron-fisted boxer, and Christian the airman far more than about my friends Rabelais and Vigny. My mother went in search of works which would restore me to my childhood: first there were '*les petits livres roses*', monthly collections of fairy-stories, and then, gradually, *Les Enfants du capitaine Grant*, *Le Dernier des Mohicans*, *Nicolas Nickleby*, and *Les Cinq sous de Lavarède*. I preferred the extravagances of Paul d'Ivoi to Jules Verne, who was too well-balanced. But who-ever the author, I adored the works in the Hetzel collection, little theatres with gold-tasselled red covers for curtains: the powdery gilding on their edges was the footlights. I owe my first experiences of beauty to these magic boxes – and not to

47

the measured phrases of Chateaubriand. When I opened them, I forgot all else: was this reading? No, it was dying of ecstasy: my self-oblivion also gave birth to natives armed with assegais, the bush, an explorer in a pith helmet. I was *vision*, and I drowned in light Aouda's handsome dark cheeks and Phinéas Fogg's side-whiskers. Freed from itself at last, the little wonder became pure wonder. Eighteen inches from the floor was born a happiness without master or yoke, complete. The New World at first seemed even more disturbing than the Old: there was plunder and killing; blood flowed freely. Indians, Hindus, Mohicans, Hottentots carried off the young girl, bound her ageing father and swore that he should die of the most horrible of tortures. It was pure Evil. But it was there only to prostrate itself at the feet of Good: in the next chapter, everything would be back to normal. Brave white men would make a hecatomb of the savages, and cut the bonds of the father who would fling himself into his daughter's arms. Only the wicked died – and a few very marginal good men, whose deaths were among the story's incidental expenses. Besides, death itself was asepticized: you fell with your arms spread wide and a small round hole under your left breast or, if guns had not been invented, the guilty men were 'put to the sword'. I liked this pretty turn of phrase: I imagined the straight white gleam of the blade; it entered as if into butter and came out through the back of the outlaw who fell to the ground without shedding a drop of blood. Sometimes death was even absurd: like that of the Saracen who, in *La Filleule de Roland*, I think, charged a crusader's horse with his own: the paladin brought his sabre down hard on the Saracen's head and sliced him from top to toe; a Gustave Doré drawing illustrated this mishap. How amusing it was! The two halves of the body, separated, began to fall, each describing a semi-circle round a stirrup; the horse reared in astonishment. For several years, I could not look at the illustration without laughing till I cried. At last I had what I needed: the Enemy, whom I could hate, but who was in the long run harmless because his schemes came to naught and even, in spite of his efforts and his devilish cunning, served the cause of Good; I realized, in fact, that a return to order was always accompanied by some form of progress: heroes were rewarded and received honours, tokens of esteem, money; thanks to their daring, a territory had been conquered, or a work of art removed from the natives and borne away to our museums; the young girl would fall in love with the explorer who had saved her life and it would all end in a marriage. From these books and magazines I derived my most personal fantasy-world: that of optimism.

This reading matter was long kept a secret; Anne-Marie had no need even to warn me: aware of their unworthiness, I did not breathe a word of them to my grandfather. I was mixing with low company, taking liberties, spending my holidays in a brothel, but I never forgot that my true self had remained in a place of worship. Why bother to shock the priest by confessing my misdeeds? Karl eventually caught me; he was angry with the two women and they, taking advantage of a moment when he paused for breath, blamed it all on me: I had seen the magazines and adventure stories, I had coveted them and asked for them – how could they refuse me? This cunning lie put my grandfather's back to the wall: it was I, I alone, who had betrayed Colomba with these over-painted wantons. I, the child prophet, the young Pythoness, the Eliakim of Belles-Lettres, was showing a mad inclination to all that was vile. It was up to the child to choose: either I stopped making prophecies or my tastes must be respected without any attempt being made to understand them. As a father, Charles Schweitzer would have burned the lot; as a grandfather, he settled for pained indulgence. I asked no more and went on quietly with my double life. It never ended: even today, I would rather read 'thrillers' than Wittgenstein.

I had been the foremost, the nonpareil of my ethereal isle; I fell to the lowest rank when I was subjected to common laws. My grandfather had decided to send me to the Lycée Montaigne. One morning, he took me along to the headmaster and extolled my merits: my only fault was to be *too* advanced for my age. The headmaster was cooperative: I was put in the *classe de huitième* and I imagined that I would be with children my own age. But no: after my first dictation, my grandfather was hastily summoned by the directors of the school. He returned home in a temper, took from his brief-case a horrid piece of paper covered with blots and scrawls, and flung it on the table: it was the paper I had handed in. They had drawn his attention to the spelling – *'le lapen çovache ême le ten*'* – and they had tried to make him realize that my place was in the *classe de dixième préparatoire*. On seeing *'lapen çovache'* my mother started to giggle; my grandfather cut her short with a terrible look. He began to accuse me of ill-will and for the first time in my life he scolded me; then he declared that I had been misunderstood; the next day, he took me away from the *lycée* and quarrelled with the headmaster.

I had not understood what was going on and my setback did not bother me: I was an infant prodigy who could not spell, that was all. And then I went back quite happily to my lonely ways: I liked what was bad for me. I had lost, without even noticing it, the chance of becoming real. Monsieur Liévin, a Parisian teacher, was engaged to give me private lessons; he came nearly every day. My grandfather had bought me a small writing-table of my own, consisting of a bench and desk of white wood. I used to sit on the bench and Monsieur Liévin would wander about giving me dictation. He looked like Vincent Auriol† and my grandfather used to insist that he was a high freemason: 'When I say good-morning to him,' he used to tell us with the disgust of a victim of a homosexual advance, 'he traces the masonic triangle with his thumb on the palm of my hand.' I hated him because he did not make a fuss of me; I think he saw me, not unreasonably, as a backward child. He disappeared. I cannot remember why: perhaps he revealed his opinion of me to someone.

We used to spend some time in Arcachon and I went to the local school there: my grandfather's democratic principles required it. But he also wanted me to be kept apart from the common herd. He handed me over to the schoolmaster with these words: 'My dear colleague, I am entrusting you with my

* *Le lapin sauvage aime le thym* (the wild rabbit likes thyme).
† President of the French Republic 1947–1954.

most precious possession.' Monsieur Barrault wore a small
beard and pince-nez: he used to come and drink muscatel at
our villa and say that he was flattered by the trust shown him
by a master at a high school. He used to make me sit at a special
desk, beside his rostrum, and, during recreation, kept me at his
side. This favouritism seemed right to me; I do not know what
my equals, the 'working-class boys', thought: I do not think
they cared. But their rowdiness wore me out and I found it
rather refined to be bored in Monsieur Barrault's vicinity while
they played prisoners' base.

I had two reasons for respecting my schoolmaster: he wished
me well and his breath smelt. Grown-ups had to be ugly,
wrinkled and disagreeable; when they clasped me, I was
offended if I did not have to overcome a slight disgust: it was
the proof that virtue was not easy. There were simple, trivial
pleasures: running, jumping, eating cakes and kissing my
mother's soft, scented skin; but I attached greater value to the
complex, studious pleasures which I experienced in the company of grown men: the repulsion with which they filled me
was part of their glamour: I confused disgust with seriousness.
I was a snob. When Monsieur Barrault leant over me, his breath
caused me delicious agony, and I eagerly inhaled the unpleas-
ing odour of his virtues. One day, I discovered a fresh piece of
writing on the wall of the School. I went over and read it: *'Le
père Barrault est un con'*. My heart pounded, I was rooted to the
spot with astonishment, and I was afraid. *'Con'*: that must be
one of those 'wicked words' which swarmed in the lower
depths of the vocabulary, and which a well-brought up child
never encountered; short and crude, it had the hideous sim-
plicity of primitive beasts. It was too much even to have read
it: I forbade myself to repeat it, even in a whisper. I did not
want this cockroach on the wall to jump into my mouth and be
changed deep down in my throat into a dark clarion-call. If I
pretended that I had not noticed it, perhaps it would go back
into a hole in the wall. But when I looked away, I kept seeing
the hateful name, *'Le père* Barrault', which upset me still more:
after all, I could only guess at the meaning of the word *'con'*;
but I was well aware to whom my family referred as *'Le père'*

So-and-So!: the gardeners, postmen, and the maid's father; poor old men, in fact. Someone saw Monsieur Barrault, the schoolmaster, my grandfather's colleague, as a poor old man. Somewhere that sick, criminal thought prowled within someone's head. Whose head? Mine, perhaps. Was it not enough to have read the blasphemous scrawl to be an accessory to a sacrilege? At the time, it seemed to me as if some cruel madman were sneering at my politeness, my respect, my eagerness, and the pleasure I took each morning in raising my cap and saying 'Good-morning, Sir', and that I myself was that madman, that the wicked words and wicked thoughts were swarming through my mind. What was to stop me, for instance, yelling at the top of my voice: 'This old tramp stinks like a pig.' I murmured: '*Le père* Barrault stinks', and everything began to spin round: I fled in tears. The very next day my deference to Monsieur Barrault and to his celluloid collar and bow-tie returned. But, when he leant over my exercise-book, I turned my head away and held my breath.

The following autumn, my mother decided to take me to the Poupon School. We had to climb a wooden staircase and enter a room on the first floor; the children arranged themselves in silence in a half-circle; seated at the far end of the room, upright and with their backs to the wall, the mothers were watching the teacher. The first duty of the poor girls who taught us was to share both praise and good marks out evenly to this academy of prodigies. If one of them showed a hint of impatience or seemed too pleased over a good answer, the Demoiselles Poupon lost pupils and she lost her post. There were a good thirty of us academicians who never even had time to speak to each other. At the exit, each mother would make a fierce grab for her child and dash off with him, without saying good-bye. After a term, my mother removed me from the class: hardly any work was done there and she had finally grown tired of feeling the weight of her neighbours' looks on her when it was my turn to be congratulated. Mademoiselle Marie-Louise, a fair-haired young girl, with pince-nez, who taught eight hours a day at the Poupons' for starvation wages, agreed to give me private lessons at home, unknown to her principals.

Sometimes she used to break off her dictation to relieve her heart with a few deep sighs: she told me that she was worn out, that she was dreadfully lonely, and that she would have given anything to have a husband, no matter whom. She, too, disappeared in the end: they made out that she taught me nothing but I suspect my grandfather thought her calamitous. This righteous man never failed to comfort the wretched but disliked having them under his roof. It was high time: Mademoiselle Marie-Louise was sapping my morale. I believed that wages were in proportion to merit and I was told that she was deserving: why then was she so badly paid? When you followed a trade, you were worthy and proud, happy to be working; since she was lucky enough to work eight hours a day, why did she always refer to her life as an incurable evil? When I passed on her complaints, my grandfather began to laugh: she was far too ugly for any man to want her. I did not laugh: could you be born condemned? In that case, I had been told lies: the order of the world concealed intolerable disorders. My concern faded as soon as she had been removed. Charles Schweitzer found me some more seemly teachers. So seemly that I have forgotten the lot of them. Until the age of ten, I was alone between one old man and two women.

My true self, my character and my name were in the hands of adults; I had learnt to see myself through their eyes; I was a child, this monster they were forming out of their regrets. When they were not there, they left their attention behind them, part of the light; I used to run and leap through this attention which preserved my status as a model grandson and which went on giving me my toys and the universe. In my pretty glass bowl, in my soul, my thoughts kept whirling, each on its own course; not a single dark corner. Yet, without words, without shape or substance, diluted in this innocent transparency, one transparent certainty spoilt everything: I was an impostor. How can you act a part without knowing it? Those bright, sunlit appearances which composed my personality gave themselves away: through a defect of being which I could neither quite understand nor stop feeling. I turned to the grown-ups, begging them to vouch for my merits: I was plunging into imposture. Condemned to please, I gave myself airs which quickly faded; I dragged my false bonhomie, my bored self-importance everywhere on the watch for some new opportunity: I thought I was grasping it, I struck a pose and once again I discovered the lack of substance from which I was trying to get away. My grandfather would drop off, wrapped in his tartan rug; under his bushy moustache, I could see his bare, pink lips; it was intolerable. Fortunately, his glasses would slip and I would rush forward to pick them up. He would wake up, lift me in his arms: we were off on our great love act: it was no longer what I had wanted. What had I wanted? I forgot everything and made my nest in the bushes of his beard. I went into the kitchen, announcing that I wanted to shake the salad; there would be cries and shrieks of laughter: 'No, darling, not like that! Hold your little hand tight: that's it! Marie, help him! Look how well he's doing it.' I was a bogus child holding a bogus salad basket; I could feel my actions changing into gestures. The Comedy detached me from men and the world: all I could see were parts and properties; since my clowning helped the activities of the grown-ups, how could I take their worries seriously? I lent myself to their schemes with a virtuous alacrity which kept me from sharing their aims. A stranger to the needs, hopes and pleasures of the human race, I squandered myself cold-bloodedly in order to seduce it; it was my audience; blazing footlights divided me from it and banished me to a proud exile which quickly turned to misery.

The worst of it was that I suspected the grown-ups of play-acting. The words they spoke to me were like sweets; but they talked to each other in a very different way. And then they sometimes broke sacred bargains: I would have on my most adorable pout, the one of which I was surest, and they would say in genuine tones: 'Go and play over there, child, we're talking.' At other times, I had the feeling that they were using me. My mother would take me to the Luxembourg Gardens and my uncle Émile, who had quarrelled with the whole family, would suddenly turn up; he would look at his sister morosely and say curtly: 'I didn't come here for your sake: it was to see the boy.' He would then explain that I was the only innocent member of the family, the only one who had never insulted him deliberately or condemned him on the strength of rumours. I would smile, embarrassed by my power and by the love which I had kindled in this gloomy man's heart. But brother and sister would already be discussing their own concerns, recapitulating their mutual grievances: Émile would fire up against Charles and Anne-Marie would defend him, giving ground; then they would go on to talk about Louise. I used to stand there between their iron chairs, forgotten. I was ready to admit – if only I had been old enough to understand them – all the right-wing truths which an old left-wing man taught me through his actions: that Truth and Myth are one and the same thing, that you have to simulate passion to feel it and that man is a creature of ceremony. I had been convinced that we were born to play-act to each other; I accepted play-acting but I insisted on taking the lead; yet, in times of crisis which left me exhausted, I noticed that I had only a bogus 'solo' part, with lines and plenty of appearances, but no scene 'of my own'; in a word, that I was supplying the grown-ups with their cues. Charles humoured me so as to wheedle death; Louise found in my liveliness a justification for her sulks, Anne-Marie for her humility. And yet, without me, my mother's parents would have given her a home, and her delicacy would have delivered her, defenceless, to Mamie; without me, Louise would have sulked, and Charles would have been filled with wonder over the Matterhorn, meteors, and other people's children. I was the opportune occasion of their differences and their reconciliations; the deeper causes were elsewhere: in Mâcon, in Gunsbach, in Thiviers, in some clogged-up ageing heart or in some past long before I was born. I reflected the unity of the family and its ancient conflicts; they were making use of my divine childhood to become what they were. I lived in a state of unease: just when their ceremonies convinced me that nothing exists without a reason and that everyone, from highest to lowest, has his appointed place in the Universe, my own *raison d'être* disappeared. I suddenly realized that I was malleable as clay, and I was ashamed of my incongruous presence in this ordered world.

A father would have ballasted me with a few lasting prejudices; creating my principles from his moods, my knowledge from his ignorance, my pride from his rancour, and my laws from his manias, he would have dwelt in me; this respectable tenant would have given me self-respect. I would have based my right to live on this respect. My begetter would have decided on my future: destined from birth to be an engineer, I should have been reassured for life. But if Jean-Baptiste Sartre had ever known my destination, he had gone off with its secret; all my mother remembered was that he had said: 'My son will not join the Navy.' Lacking more precise information, no one, beginning with myself, knew what the hell I had come on earth to do. If he had left me some property, my childhood would have been altered; I should not write because I should be someone else. Lands and a house give a young heir a stable image of himself; he is aware of himself on *his* drive and in the leaded window-panes of *his* verandah, and creates, out of their inertia, the immortal substance of his soul. A few days ago, in a restaurant, the proprietor's son, a small boy of seven, shouted to the woman at the cash-desk: 'When my father's not here, I'm the Master.' There's a man for you! At his age, I was no one's master and nothing belonged to me. In my rare moments of frivolity, my mother would whisper to me: 'Careful! We aren't at home!' We were never at home: either in the rue le Goff or later on, when my mother remarried. I did not suffer through this, since everything was lent to me; but I remained an abstraction. To an owner, this world's goods reflect what he is; they taught me what I was not. *I was not* stable or permanent; *I was not* the perpetuator-to-be of my father's work; *I was not* necessary to the production of steel; in short, I had no soul.

This would have been fine if I had got on all right with my body. But it and myself formed an odd couple. A poor child does not question itself: ravaged *bodily* by want and sickness, its unjustifiable condition justifies its existence. Hunger and the constant danger of death are the bases of its right to live: it lives so as not to die. But I was not rich enough to consider myself predestined or poor enough for my envious wishes to be exigent. I fulfilled my alimentary duties and God some-times – rarely – sent me that grace which permits you to eat without disgust – appetite. Breathing, digesting, defecating listlessly, I went on living because I had begun to live. I was unaware of the violence and fierce cravings of that forcibly fed companion, my body: it brought itself to my attention by a series of cosy illnesses, greatly encouraged by the grown-ups. At the time, a refined family had to include at least one delicate child. I was the perfect subject because I had had some thought of dying at birth. They kept a watch on me, felt my pulse, took my temperature, and made me stick out my tongue. 'Don't you think he's rather pale?' 'It's the light.' 'I'm quite sure he's got thinner!' 'But, papa, we weighed him yesterday.' Beneath these searching looks, I felt myself become an object, a potted plant. Eventually, I would be bundled into bed. Suffocated by the heat as I simmered between the sheets, I confused my body with its sickness: I no longer knew which of the two was undesirable.

Monsieur Simonnot, my grandfather's collaborator, used to lunch with us on Thursdays. I envied this fifty-year-old man with girlish cheeks who waxed his moustache and dyed his forelock: when Anne-Marie asked him, to keep the conversa-tion going, if he liked Bach, if he enjoyed being by the sea or in the mountains, if he had happy memories of his native town, he would pause for thought and let his mind dwell on the granite-like mountain-range of his tastes. When he had ob-tained the required information, he would communicate it to my mother in a detached tone, nodding his head. What a happy man he must be!, I thought, to wake up joyfully each morning and survey, from some Sublime Point, his peaks, ridges, and valleys, and then stretch himself pleasurably as he said: 'This is me all right: I am Monsieur Simonnot whole and entire.' Naturally, I was able, when asked, to make known my prefer-ences and even to insist on them; but when I was alone, they escaped me: far from being sure of them, I had to grip them, push them, breathe life into them; I was no longer even sure if I preferred beefsteak to roast veal. I would have given anything for some tortured landscape, with prejudices sheer as cliffs, to be installed in me. When Madame Picard, tactfully using fashionable expressions, said of my grandfather: 'Charles is an exquisite person', or 'One can't know a person', I felt condemned without appeal. The stones in the Luxembourg Gardens, Monsieur Simonnot, the chestnut trees and Karlémami were all beings. I was not. I had not got their inertia, their depth, or their inscrutability. I was *nothing*: an indelible transparency. My jealousy knew no limits the day that I was told that Monsieur Simonnot, that statue, that monolithic block, was, into the bargain, indispensable to the universe.

It was an occasion. At the Institute for Modern Languages, the crowd was clapping its hands beneath the flickering light of a gas-mantle, my mother was playing Chopin and everyone, at my grandfather's orders, was talking French: a slow, guttural French, with faded graces and the pomp of an oratorio. I flew from hand to hand without touching ground; I was suffocating against the bosom of a German woman novelist when my grandfather, from the height of his glory, made a pronouncement which pierced me to the heart: 'Someone's lacking here: it's Simonnot.' I fled from the novelist's arms, took refuge in a corner, and the guests disappeared; in the centre of a tumultuous circle, I saw a pillar: Monsieur Simonnot himself, absent in flesh and blood. This astonishing absence transfigured him. A great many people connected with the Institute were absent: some pupils were sick, others had sent their excuses; but these were merely accidental and trifling facts. Only Monsieur Simonnot was *lacking*. It had been enough to mention his name: emptiness had sunk into that crowded hall like a knife. I was amazed that a man had his place fixed. His place: a void hollowed out by universal expectation, an invisible womb from which it seemed one could suddenly be reborn. Yet, if he had sprung from the ground, to a general ovation, and even if the women had flung themselves at him and kissed his hand, I should have come to my senses: physical presence is always excessive. Virgin, reduced to the purity of a negative

58

essence, he preserved the hard transparency of a diamond. As it was my private lot to be situated the whole time among certain people, in a certain part of the earth, and to know that I was superfluous, I wanted to be missed, like water, bread, or air, by everyone else in every other place.

This wish returned to my lips each day. Charles Schweitzer was everywhere compelled to dissimulate an anguish which I never noticed while he lived and which I am only beginning to suspect. All his colleagues bore the sky on their shoulders. Among these Atlases were grammarians, philologists and linguists, Monsieur Lyon-Caen, and the editor of the *Revue pédagogique*. He referred to them sententiously to make us appreciate their importance: 'Lyon-Caen knows his business. His place is at the Institut de France,' or: 'Shurer makes out he's getting on; let's hope they won't be foolish enough to let him retire: the Faculty doesn't know what it would be losing.' Surrounded by irreplaceable old men whose impending disappearance would plunge Europe into mourning and possibly into barbarism, I would have given anything to hear an incredible voice pass judgement in my heart: 'This young Sartre knows his business; if he should disappear, France doesn't know what it would be losing!' A bourgeois childhood is spent in the eternity of the moment, that is to say in inactivity; I wanted to be Atlas straight away, for ever, and since the beginning of time. It did not occur to me that you could work to become one; I needed a Supreme Court or a decree to restore my rights to me. But where were the magistrates? My natural judges were disqualified by their playacting; I objected to them, but I could see no others.

Stunned vermin, without law or faith, reason or goal, I took refuge in the family comedy, whirling, running, flying from one deception to another. I fled from my unjustifiable body and its shabby secrets; when the top ran into an obstacle and stopped, the pallid little actor withdrew into an animal stupor. Good friends told my mother that I was sad, and that they had caught me dreaming. My mother hugged me to her with a laugh: 'You're so cheerful, always singing! What could you feel unhappy about? You have everything you want.' She was right: a spoilt child is not sad: he is bored, like a king. Or like a dog.

I was a dog: I yawned, the tears flowed, I could feel them flowing. I was a tree and the wind clung to my branches and made them stir vaguely. I was a fly; I climbed all the way up a window-pane, slid down, and started to climb again. Sometimes I felt the caress of time passing; at others – more frequent – I felt it did not pass. Tremulous moments got stuck, swallowed me up and would not end their dying; stagnant but still alive, they were swept away. Others took their place, fresher but as pointless. These disappointments are called happiness; my mother kept telling me I was the happiest of small boys. How could I not believe her *since it was true*? I never thought myself neglected; for one thing, there is no word to describe it; and then I do not see it: I was always surrounded. This was the web of my life, the stuff of my pleasures, the flesh of my thoughts.

I saw death. At the age of five: it was watching me; in the evenings, it prowled on the balcony: it pressed its nose to the window; I used to see it but I did not dare to say anything. Once, on the Quai Voltaire, we met it: it was a tall, mad old woman, dressed in black, who mumbled as she went by: 'I shall put that child in my pocket.' Another time, it took the form of a hole: this was at Arcachon; Karlémami and my mother were visiting Madame Dupont and her son Gabriel, the composer. I was playing in the garden of the villa, scared because I had been told that Gabriel was ill and was going to die. I was playing at horses, half-heartedly, and galloping round the house. Suddenly, I noticed a gloomy hole: the cellar, which had been opened; an indescribable impression of loneliness and horror blinded me: I turned round and, singing at the top of my voice, I fled. At that time, I had an assignation with it every night in my bed. It was a ritual: I had to sleep on my left side, my face to the wall; I would wait, trembling all over, and it would appear, a very conventional skeleton, with a scythe; I then had permission to turn on my right side, it would go away and I could sleep in peace. In the daytime, I used to recognize it in the most varied disguises: if my mother happened to sing *Le*

Roi des Aulnes in French, I would stop my ears; after reading *L'Ivrogne et sa femme*, I went six months without opening La Fontaine's fables. The old hag did not care: hidden in a Mérimée short story, *La Vénus d'Ille*, she waited until I was reading it to spring at my throat. Burials did not worry me nor did tombs; about this time, my grandmother Sartre fell ill and died; summoned by telegram, my mother and I reached Thiviers while she was still alive. It was decided to send me away from the place where her long and unhappy life was drawing to its close; friends took charge of me, had me to stay, and kept me occupied with instructive games, invented for the occasion and invested with a funerary atmosphere by boredom. I played, read and took pains to show an exemplary attitude, but I felt nothing. Not even when we followed the hearse to the cemetery. Death was conspicuous by its absence: to pass away was not to die, and the transformation of that old woman into a tombstone did not displease me; there was transubstantiation and accession to being; everything, in fact, happened as if I had been transformed, ceremonially, into Monsieur Simonnot. For this reason, I have always liked, and still do, Italian cemeteries: the stone is tortured into some sort of baroque figure, and a medallion is set into it containing a photo recalling the dead person as he was in his former state. When I was seven, I met true Death, Grim Death, everywhere, but never there. What was it? A person and a threat. The person was mad; as for the threat, it was like this: dark mouths might open anywhere, in broad daylight or in the brightest sunshine, and snap me up. There was a horrible reverse to things, and when you lost your reason, you saw it; dying was carrying madness to extremes and being swallowed up in it. I lived in terror – it was a genuine neurosis. If I seek its cause, it goes like this: a spoilt child, a providential gift, I found my profound uselessness even more obvious because the family ritual struck me persistently as a contrived necessity. I felt superfluous so I had to disappear. I was a sickly bloom under constant sentence of extinction. In other words, I was condemned, and the sentence could be carried out at any time. Yet I rejected it with all my strength: not that my life was dear to me – quite the contrary, for I did not cling to it: the more absurd life is, the less tolerable death.

God would have got me out of difficulty: I would have been a signed masterpiece; confident of playing my part in the universal chorus, I would have waited patiently for Him to reveal His designs and my need. I was aware of religion, I hoped for it, and it was the remedy. If it had been kept from me, I should have invented it myself. It was not kept from me: brought up in the Catholic faith, I learnt that the Almighty had made me to his greater glory: it was more than I dared to dream. But, as a result, I did not recognize in the fashionable God that was taught me Him who was waiting for my soul. I needed a Creator – I was given a Big Businessman. The two were one, but I did not realize it; I served the pharisaic Idol unenthusiastically and the official doctrine disgusted me with the idea of seeking my own faith. What luck! Trust and desolation made of my soul a chosen soil in which to sow heaven; without this misunderstanding, I should have been a monk. But my family had been affected by the slow dechristianization which was born in the Voltaire-influenced *haute bourgeoisie* and took a century to spread to every stratum of Society: without this general slackening of faith, Louise Guillemin, a young Catholic lady from the provinces, would have made more fuss about marrying a Lutheran. Naturally, everyone at home believed: for reasons of discretion. Seven or eight years after the Combes ministry,* avowed unbelief still had all the violence and anarchy of a passion; an atheist was an eccentric, a hot-head whom you did not invite to dinner lest he 'create a scandal', a fanatic burdened with taboos who denied himself the right to kneel in church, to marry his daughters or indulge in tears there, who took it on himself to prove the truth of his doctrine by the purity of his conduct, who injured himself and his happiness to the extent of robbing himself of his means of dying comforted, a man with a phobia about God who saw his absence everywhere and who could not open his mouth without saying His name: in short, a Gentleman with religious

* Émile Combes (1835–1921), French prime minister 1902–5, noted for his anticlericalism.

convictions. The believer had none: for two thousand years the Christian certainties had had time to prove themselves, they belonged to everyone, and they were required to shine in a priest's glance, in the half-light of a church, and to illumine souls, but no one needed to appropriate them to himself; they were the common patrimony. Polite Society believed in God so that it need not talk of Him. How tolerant religion seemed! How convenient it was: the Christian could abandon Mass and yet marry his children in church, smile at the religious 'art' of the place Saint-Sulpice and shed tears as he listened to the Wedding March from Lohengrin; he was not obliged to lead an exemplary life or to die in despair, or even to have himself cremated. In our circle, in my family, faith was nothing but an official name for sweet French liberty; I had been baptized, like so many others, to preserve my independence: in refusing me baptism, they would have been afraid of doing harm to my soul; as a registered Catholic, I was free, I was normal. 'Later on,' they said, 'he can do as he pleases.' It was reckoned, at the time, far harder to acquire faith than to lose it.

Charles Schweitzer was too much of a performer not to need a Great Spectator but he hardly ever thought about God except at peak moments; confident of meeting Him in the hour of death, he kept Him apart from his life. In private, out of loyalty to our lost provinces, and to the coarse delight of his anti-papist brethren, he never missed an opportunity of poking fun at Catholicism: his Table Talk was like Luther's. He talked endlessly about Lourdes: Bernadette had seen 'some worthy woman changing her vest', a paralysed man had been plunged into the swimming-bath and, when he had been brought out, 'he could see with both eyes'. He told the story of Saint Labre, covered with fleas, and of Saint Marie Alacoque, who cleaned up the excrement of the sick with her tongue. These tall stories helped me: I became even more inclined to set myself up above worldly possessions, of which I had none, and I would have found my vocation without difficulty in my comfortable penury; mysticism suits displaced persons and superfluous children: to plunge me into it, it would have been enough to show me the question from the other side; I was in danger of

being a victim of saintliness. My grandfather disgusted me with
it for good: I saw it through his eyes, and this cruel folly sickened me with its mawkish ecstasies and terrified me with its
sadistic contempt for the body; the eccentricities of the Saints
had little more meaning than that of the Englishman who dived
into the sea in a dinner jacket. When listening to these tales, my
grandmother would make a show of protest, call her husband
'unbeliever' and 'heretic', and rap him over the knuckles, but
the indulgence in her smile was enough to disillusion me; she
believed in nothing; only her scepticism kept her from being
an atheist. My mother was very careful not to interfere; she
had 'her private God' and asked little more of Him than to
comfort her in secret. The debate continued, more feebly, in
my brain: another self, my dark brother, languidly challenged
every one of the articles of faith; I was both Catholic and
Protestant and I united the spirit of criticism with that of sub-
mission. Deep down, it all bored me to death; I was led to
unbelief not through conflicting dogma but through my grandparents' indifference. Yet I believed: in my nightshirt, kneeling
on my bed, hands folded, I said my daily prayer but thought
less and less often about the good God. On Thursdays, my
mother took me to the Abbé Dibildos's school. I went to a
religious class there among children I did not know. My grandfather had done his job so well that I thought the priests an odd
lot; although they heard *my* confession, they were more alien
to me than pastors, because of their dress and their celibacy.
Charles Schweitzer respected the Abbé Dibildos – 'a decent
fellow!' – whom he knew personally, but his anticlericalism
was so outspoken that I went through the gateway with the
feeling that I was crossing into enemy territory. I did not, personally, dislike priests: when they spoke to me they put on the
gentle expression, massaged by spirituality, the air of benign
wonder and the far-away look which I particularly liked in
Madame Picard and other old women musician friends of my
mother's; it was my grandfather who loathed them through
me. It was he who first had the idea of entrusting me to his
friend, the Abbé, but he used to scrutinize with anxiety the
little Catholic that was brought back to him on Thursday even-

64

ings; he would search in my eyes for the advance of popery and did not scruple to chaff me. This uneasy situation lasted no more than six months. One day, I handed my teacher a French essay on the Passion; it had delighted my family, and my mother had copied it out herself. It won only the silver medal. This disappointment plunged me into impiety. An illness and the holidays prevented me from going back to the Dibildos school; when term began again, I refused to return there. For several years longer, I kept up public relations with the Almighty; in private, I stopped associating with Him. Once only I had the feeling that He existed. I had been playing with matches and had burnt a mat; I was busy covering up my crime when suddenly God saw me. I felt His gaze inside my head and on my hands; I turned round and round in the bathroom, horribly visible, a living target. I was saved by indignation: I grew angry at such a crude lack of tact, and blasphemed, muttering like my grandfather: '*Sacré nom de Dieu de nom de Dieu de nom de Dieu.*' He never looked at me again.

I have just told the story of a missed vocation; I needed God, he was given to me, and I received him without understanding what I was looking for. Unable to take root in my heart, he vegetated in me for a while and then died. Today, when He is mentioned, I say with the amusement and lack of regret of some ageing beau who meets an old flame: 'Fifty years ago, without that misunderstanding, without that mistake, without the accident which separated us, there might have been something between us.'

Nothing happened between us. Yet my affairs went from bad to worse. My grandfather was irritated by my long hair. 'He's a boy,' he used to say to my mother. 'You're making a girl of him; I don't want my grandson to be a milksop!' Anne-Marie held out; she would, I think, have liked me to be a real girl; she would have loved to lavish kindnesses on an echo of her own sad childhood. Heaven had not granted her prayers, so she made the best of it. I was to have the sex of the angels, indeterminate but feminine round the edges. An affectionate woman, she taught me affection; my loneliness did the rest and kept me away from rough games. One day – I was seven – my

grandfather had had enough: he took me by the hand, saying
that he was taking me for a walk. But no sooner had we turned
the corner of the road than he thrust me into the hairdresser's,
saying: 'We'll give your mother a surprise.' I adored surprises.
They were always happening at home. Mysteries, sometimes
amusing, sometimes full of virtue, unexpected presents,
dramatic revelations followed by hugs and kisses: that was the
tenor of our life. When I had my appendix out, my mother did
not breathe a word to Karl, to spare him the anxiety which he
would certainly not have felt. My uncle Auguste had provided
the money; we returned in secret from Arcachon and went into
hiding in a nursing-home at Courbevoie. Two days after the
operation, Auguste went to see my grandfather: 'I've some good
news for you,' he announced. Karl was taken in by the friendly
gravity of his voice: 'You're marrying again!' 'No,' replied my
uncle with a smile, 'but everything went very well.' 'What do
you mean, everything?' etc., etc. In short, melodrama was my
staple diet and I watched with equanimity as my curls slid
down the white towel round my neck and dropped to the floor,
inexplicably dull; I went home proud and shorn.

There were exclamations but no hugs and kisses, and my
mother shut herself up in her bedroom to weep: her little girl
had been changed into a little boy. There was worse to come:
while my pretty curls waved round my ears, she had been able
to deny the existence of my ugliness. Yet my right eye was
already on the way to semi-darkness. She had to admit the truth
to herself. Even my grandfather seemed quite taken aback: he
had gone out with his wonder child and had brought home a
toad: he had undermined the foundations for future marvel-
lings. Mamie looked at him in amusement. All she said was:
'Karl's not proud of himself; he's showing he feels guilty.'

Anne-Marie was kind enough to hide from me why she was
upset. I did not find out until I was twelve, and then roughly.
But I felt ill at ease. I often caught glances of surprise or puzzle-
ment cast in my direction by friends of the family. My audience
grew less responsive each day; I had to make an effort; I laboured
my effects and began to overact. I went through the agonies
of an ageing actress: I discovered that others could please.

Two memories remain, from somewhat later; they were shattering.

I was nine, and it was raining. There were ten of us children in the hotel at Noirétable, ten cats in one bag; to keep us busy, my grandfather agreed to write and produce a patriotic play for ten characters. Bernard the eldest of the group, was Old Struthoff, a benevolent curmudgeon. I was a young Alsatian; my father had opted for France and I was crossing the frontier, in secret, to go and join him. I had been provided with some defiant dialogue: I extended my right arm, lowered my head and muttered, hiding my smooth cheek in the hollow of my shoulder: '*Adieu, adieu, notre chère Alsace.*' At rehearsals they said I was perfectly sweet; this did not surprise me. The performance took place in the garden. Two clumps of spindle trees and the wall of the hotel marked the bounds of the stage; the parents were sitting on cane chairs. The children enjoyed themselves like mad; except me. Convinced that the fate of the play lay in my hands, I did all I could to please, through devotion to the common cause; I believed all eyes were fixed on me. I went too far; all votes went to Bernard, who was less mannered. Did I realize? After the performance, he took up a collection: I slipped behind him and tugged at his beard which came away in my hand. It was a star actor's whimsy, just a joke; I was delighted with myself and hopped from one foot to the other, brandishing my trophy. No one laughed. My mother took me by the hand and quickly drew me aside: 'What's the matter with you?' she asked, hurt to the quick. 'It was such a lovely beard! Everyone cried out in surprise.' My grandmother had already joined us with the latest news: Bernard's mother had said something about jealousy. 'You see what happens when you show off!' I escaped, and ran to our bedroom, where I stood in front of the wardrobe mirror and spent a long time making faces.

Madame Picard believed that a child should be allowed to read anything: 'A book never does any harm if it is well written.' While she was there, I had once asked permission to read *Madame Bovary* and my mother, in an oversweet voice, had said: 'But if my little darling reads books like that at his age, what will he do when he grows up?' 'I shall live them!' This reply had met with the most complete and lasting success. Each time she called on us, Madame Picard would refer to it and my mother, flattered, would scold her: 'Blanche! Will you be quiet, you'll spoil him!' I liked and despised this pale, fat old woman, my best audience; when I was told that she was to visit us, I felt I had genius: I dreamt that she lost her skirts and that I saw her bottom, which was a way of paying tribute to her wit. In November 1915, she made me a present of a red leather book, with gilt-edged leaves. We were sitting, my grandfather being away, in his study; the women were talking animatedly but rather more quietly than in 1914, because of the war. A dirty, yellow fog, smelling of stale tobacco-smoke, was pressing against the windows. I opened the book and was at first disappointed: I was expecting a novel or some short stories; on its multi-coloured pages I read the same questionnaire twenty times over. 'Fill it in,' she said to me, 'and get your little friends to fill it in: you'll be storing up happy memories for yourself.' I realized that I was being offered a chance to be wonderful: I wanted to answer at once, sat down at my grandfather's desk, laid the book on the blotting-paper of his blotter, picked up his galalith penholder, dipped the nib into the bottle of red ink, and began to write while the grown-ups exchanged amused glances. In an instant, I was altogether above myself in the quest for 'answers in advance of my age'. Unfortunately, the questionnaire did not help me; it examined me as to my likes and dislikes: what was my favourite colour, my favourite perfume? I was idly devising my preferences when the chance to shine presented itself: 'What is your dearest wish?' I replied without hesitation: 'To be a soldier and avenge the dead.' Then, too excited to go on, I came down to earth and took my work over to the grown-ups. Their eyes brightened, Madame Picard adjusted her spectacles and my mother leant on her shoulder; both began to purse their lips unkindly. They looked up together: my mother was pink in the face. Madame Picard handed the book back to me: 'You know, my young friend, it's interesting only if you really mean it.' I thought I would die. My mistake was patent: they wanted the infant prodigy, and I had given them the child sublime. Unfortunately for me, neither of them had anyone at the front: my sublime soldier had no effect on their tolerant souls. I disappeared, and went and made faces in front of a mirror. When I recall those grimaces today, I realize that they were a form of self-protection. I was guarding myself against the lightning flashes of shame by a barrier of muscle. And then, by carrying my misfortune to extremes, they freed me from it: I plunged into humility to evade humiliation. I got rid of my means of pleasing so as to forget that I had had them and had misused them; the mirror was a great help to me: I gave it the job of teaching me that I was a monster; if it succeeded, my bitter remorse would turn to pity. But, most important, the failure having revealed my servility to me, I uglified myself to make my slavishness impossible, to renounce men, and have them renounce me. The Comedy of Evil was being played against the Comedy of Good; Eliakim was acting the part of Quasimodo. By screwing and wrinkling it up, I was altering my face; I was throwing acid at myself to efface my old smiles.

The remedy was worse than the disease: I had tried to take refuge from glory and dishonour in the loneliness of my true self; but I had no true self: I found nothing within me except a surprised insipidity. Before my eyes, a jellyfish was striking against the glass of the aquarium, feebly gathering its ruffle and fraying into the shadows. Night fell and inky clouds invaded the mirror, burying my final incarnation. Deprived of an alibi, I fell back on myself. In the darkness, I sensed a vague hesitation, a rustling, a banging noise, a whole living creature – most terrifying and the only thing of which I could not be afraid. I fled; and in the light resumed my role of tarnished cherub. In vain. The mirror had told me what I had always known: I was horribly ordinary. I have never got over it.

Idolized by all, but rejected individually, I was an item that had been returned, and, at the age of seven, I could fall back only on myself; who did not yet exist. I was an empty palace of mirrors in which the emergent century reflected its boredom. I had been born to satisfy the great need I had of myself; until then I had known only the vanities of a lap-dog. Face to face with pride, I became the Proud One. Since no one claimed me *seriously*, I set up the pretension that I was indispensable to the Universe. What more lofty? What more absurd? In fact, I had no choice. Stowaway traveller, I had fallen asleep on the seat and the ticket-inspector was shaking me. 'Your ticket!' I was forced to admit that I had not got one. Or the money to defray the cost of the journey there and then. I began by pleading guilty: I had left my identity papers at home and I could no longer remember how I had managed to get past the ticket-puncher, but I admitted that I had entered the carriage on false pretences. So far from challenging the ticket-inspector's authority, I protested aloud my respect for his position and submitted in advance to his decision. At this pole of humility, I could save myself only by reversing the situation; so I revealed that I was summoned to Dijon by important and secret reasons which concerned France and possibly humanity. Looked at in this new light, there was no one to be found in the whole train with as much right to occupy a seat in it as myself. Naturally, it was a question of a superior law which conflicted with the regulations but, in taking it on himself to interrupt my journey, the ticket-inspector would be provoking serious complications the consequences of which would rebound on his head. I pleaded with him to think it over: was it rational to will the entire race to chaos on the grounds of maintaining order in a train? Such is pride: the wretch's defence. Only travellers with tickets have the right to be modest. I never knew if I won my case: the ticket-inspector said nothing. I began my explanations over again; while I kept talking, I felt sure that he would not make me get off the train. We remained face to face, the one silent, the other indefatigable, as the train bore us towards Dijon. The train, the ticket-inspector, and the culprit were myself. And I was also a fourth character; he, the organizer, had only one wish: to be taken in, if only for a minute, and to forget that he had started the whole thing. The family comedy helped me: I was called a gift from heaven for a joke, and I was not unaware of this; overfed with affection, I cried easily but my heart was cold: I wanted to become a present useful to the researches of those for whom it was intended; I offered up my person to France and to the world. I did not give a damn for people, but, since I had to be among them, their tears of joy would make it clear to me that the universe welcomed me with gratitude. I may be thought presumptuous; no: I was a fatherless child. No man's son, I was my own cause, acme of pride and acme of wretchedness; I had been sent into the world by the force which was carrying me towards good. The chain seemed clear: made feminine through the fondness of my mother, flavourless through the absence of the severe Moses who had begotten me, and eaten up with conceit through my grandfather's adoration, I was pure object, doomed, above all, to masochism, had I only been able to believe in the family comedy. But I could not; it affected me only superficially, and deep down I remained cold, unjustified; the system horrified me, and I began to loathe my happy swoons, my lack of reserve, my over-fondled, over-tended body; I discovered myself through opposition and flung myself into pride and sadism, otherwise known as generosity. This last, like greed or racialism, is merely a balm secreted as a cure for our inner wounds which, in the end, poisons us: to escape the desolation of created things, I prepared for myself the middle-class solitude for which there is no cure: that of the creator. This change of tack must not be taken as a genuine revolt: you rebel against a tyrant, and I had only benefactors. I remained their accomplice a long while. After all, it was they who had christened me a gift of Providence: all I did was use to other ends the instruments at my disposal.

Everything took place in my head; an imaginary child, I protected myself through the imagination. When I recall my life from six to nine, I am struck by the continuity of my spiritual exercises. They often altered in content but the programme did not vary; I had made a false entrance, so I retired behind a screen and started my birth over again at a selected point, at the very moment that the universe was silently crying out for me.

My first stories were simply replicas of The Bluebird, Puss-in-Boots, and Maurice Bouchor's tales. They repeated themselves singly, behind my forehead, between my eyebrows.

Later on, I went so far as to touch them up, to play a part in them. They changed in nature; I did not like fairies, there were too many around me: exploits took the place of fairyland. I became a hero; I stripped myself bare of charm; it was no longer a question of giving pleasure but of dominating. I abandoned my family: Karlémami and Anne-Marie were excluded from my fantasies. Sated with gestures and attitudes, I performed real actions in my dreams. I invented a harsh and deadly universe – that of Cri-Cri, L'Épatant, and Paul d'Ivoi; – and in the place of need and work, of which I knew nothing, I put danger. I was never further from challenging the established order: confident I was living in the best of worlds, I undertook to purge it of its monsters; policeman and lyncher, I offered up a gang of brigands in sacrifice every evening. I did not make any preventive wars or punitive expeditions; I killed without pleasure or anger in order to snatch young girls from death. These frail creatures were indispensable to me: they would cry out for me. Obviously they could not count on my help because they did not know me. But I flung them into such great dangers that no one could have rescued them except myself. When the janissaries brandished their curved scimitars, a groan would run through the desert and the rocks would say to the sand: 'Someone's lacking here: it's Sartre.' Just then, I would draw aside the screen, send heads flying with a few strokes of my sabre, and be born in a welter of blood. The joy of cold steel! I was in my element!

I was born in order to die: saved, the girl would fling herself into the arms of the margrave, her father; I would go away: I must either become superfluous again, or seek out fresh murderers. I found them. Champion of the established order, I had placed my *raison d'être* in perpetual chaos; I would suffocate Evil in my arms, I would die with its death, recover with its resurrection. I was a right-wing anarchist. Nothing came of this well-meaning violence; I remained servile and zealous: the habit of virtue is not so easily lost; but, every evening, I would wait impatiently till the daily clowning was over, rush to my bed, gabble my prayers and slip between my sheets; I could not wait to get back to my mad audacity. I would age in the darkness and become a lonely adult, with neither father nor mother, hearth nor home, almost without a name. I would walk across a blazing roof, carrying a fainting woman in my arms; below me, the crowd would be shouting: it was obvious the building was about to crumble. At this point, I would say aloud the prophetic words: 'To be continued.' 'What do you say?' my mother would ask. I would reply, prudently: 'I'm holding myself in suspense.' And the fact is that I did go to sleep, in the throes of danger and in a state of delightful uncertainty. The following evening, keeping my appointment, I would be back with my roof, the flames and certain death. Suddenly, I would notice a gutter which I had not observed the previous evening. Saved, by God! But how could I hang from it without letting go of my precious burden? Luckily, the young woman would recover her senses, I would take her on my back and she would clasp her arms round my neck. No, on second thoughts, I would plunge her back into unconsciousness: however little she had contributed to her rescue, my merit would be diminished by that much. By chance, there would be this rope at my feet: I would bind the victim firmly to her rescuer and the rest would be child's play. Some Gentlemen – the mayor, the chief of police, and the captain of the fire brigade – would catch me in their arms, embrace me, and give me a medal. I would lose my confidence; I would not know what more to do with myself: the embraces of these dignitaries would be too like my grandfather's. I would wipe the slate clean and begin again: it was night, a young girl was calling for help, and I would dash into the affray. . . . *To be continued in our next.* I would risk my life for the sublime moment which would change a roaming creature into a heaven-sent passer-by, but I felt I should not survive my victory and I was too happy to put it off until the following day.

It may be surprising to meet these rakehell fantasies in a scribbler destined for priesthood; children's anxieties are metaphysical; there is no need to shed blood to appease them. Did I, then, never wish to be a heroic doctor and save my fellow-citizens from bubonic plague or cholera? Never, I must confess. Yet I was neither savage nor warlike and it is not my fault if the emergent century gave me an epic turn of mind. Defeated, France was swarming with imaginary heroes whose exploits salved its self-respect. Eight years before my birth, Cyrano de Bergerac had 'burst out like a fanfare of red trousers'. A little later, *L'Aiglon*, proud and battered, had only to appear to efface Fashoda.* In 1912, I knew nothing of these noble characters but I was in constant touch with their derivatives: I adored the Cyrano of the Underworld, Arsène Lupin, without realizing that he owed his herculean strength, his shrewd courage, his typically French intelligence to our being caught with our pants down in 1870. National aggressiveness and the spirit of revenge made all children avengers. I became an avenger like everyone else: attracted by the banter, the flamboyance, the intolerable faults of the defeated, I jeered at the ruffians before I broke their backs. But wars bored me. I liked the easygoing Germans who used to visit my grandfather and I was interested only in private injustices; collective forces became transformed in my heart that knew no hate: I used them to nourish my personal heroism. No matter: I am branded: if, in an iron century, I committed the foolish blunder of mistaking life for an epic, it was because I was the grandchild of defeat. A convinced materialist, my epic idealism will make amends, until my death, for an insult I have not endured, a shame I have not suffered, and the loss of two provinces which have been given back to us long since.

The bourgeois of the last century never forgot their first evening in the theatre, and their writers made it their business to describe the occasion. When the curtain rose, the children thought they were at court. The golds and purples, the bright lights, the make-up, the emphasis and artifice endowed even crime with sacredness; on the stage they saw the resurrection of the nobility which their grandfathers had murdered. In the intervals, the tiers of balconies presented them with a picture

* Anglo-French incident in the Sudan, 1898, when Major (afterwards General) Marchand occupied Fashoda on the White Nile, but withdrew a month later following negotiations between the French and British governments.

of society; in the boxes they could observe bare shoulders and and living noblemen. They returned home, stunned, softened, insidiously prepared for ceremonious destinies, ready to be-become Jules Favre, Jules Ferry or Jules Grévy.* I challenge my contemporaries to tell me the date of their first experience of the cinema. We entered blindly into a traditionless century which was to contrast sharply with the others by its bad manners, and the new plebeian art anticipated our barbarism. Born in a robber's cave, classified by the authorities along with travelling entertainers, it had certain vulgar qualities which shocked serious people; it was an amusement for women and children. My mother and I adored it, but we hardly ever thought about it and we never mentioned it: do you mention bread if there is plenty of it? When we became aware of its existence, it had long since become our major need.

On rainy days, Anne-Marie would ask me what I wanted to do, and we would hesitate a long while between the circus, the Châtelet, the Maison Électrique, and the Musée Grévin; at the last moment, with deliberate casualness, we would decide to go to a picture theatre. My grandfather would appear at the door of his study when we opened the door of the flat; he would ask: 'Where are you children off to?' 'To the cinema,' my mother would say. He would frown and she would add hastily: 'To the Panthéon cinema, it's very near; we only have to cross the rue Soufflot.' He would let us go with a shrug; the following Thursday, he would say to Monsieur Simonnot: 'Look here, Simonnot, you're a sensible fellow, can you understand this? My daughter takes my grandson to the cinema!' and Monsieur Simonnot would say in a conciliatory tone: 'I've never been but my wife sometimes goes.'

The show would have begun. As we stumbled along behind the attendant, I felt I was there surreptitiously; above our heads, a beam of white light would be shining across the hall, and dust and smoke would be dancing in it; a piano would be tinkling, violet light-bulbs would be glowing on the wall, and I would catch my breath at the varnish-like smell of a disinfectant. The smell and the fruits of that inhabited night mingled within me:

* French statesmen of the nineteenth century.

75

I was eating the exit lights, filling myself with their acid taste. I would scrape my back against people's knees, sit on a creaking seat. My mother slipped a folded rug under my buttocks to raise me up; finally I would look at the screen and would see fluorescent chalk, and shimmering landscapes streaked with rain; it was always raining, even in bright sunshine, even inside a flat; sometimes a fiery planet would cross a baroness's drawing-room without her appearing to be surprised. I used to love that rain, that restless disquiet which tormented the wall. The pianist would strike up the overture to *Fingal's Cave* and everyone would know that the villain was about to appear: the baroness would be crazed with terror. But her handsome, dusky face would be replaced by a mauve notice: 'End of first part.' Then would come the abrupt sobering-up and the lights. Where was I? At school? In a government office? No ornaments of any kind: rows of tip-up seats which revealed their springs when pushed up, walls smeared with ochre, and a wooden floor littered with cigarette ends and spittle. Muffled voices would fill the hall, words would exist once more; the attendant would offer boiled sweets for sale and my mother would buy me some; I would put them in my mouth and I was sucking the exit lights. People would rub their eyes and everyone would realize he had neighbours. Soldiers, local servants; a bony old man would be chewing, hatless working-women would be laughing out loud: all these people were not of our world. Fortunately, dotted here and there in this parterre of heads, large bobbing hats brought reassurance.

The social hierarchy of the theatre had given my late father and my grandfather, who used to sit in the upper circle, a taste for ceremony: when a lot of men get together, they have to be separated by rituals or else they slaughter each other. The cinema proved the opposite: the very mixed audience seemed to have been united by a disaster rather than by a show; once dead, etiquette finally unmasked the true link between men, their adhesion. I came to loathe ceremonies but I adored crowds; I have seen all kinds, but I never recovered that naked awareness without recoil of each individual towards all the others, that waking dream, that obscure awareness of the danger of being a man until 1940, in Stalag XII D.

My mother even went so far as to take me to the Boulevard cinemas: the Kinérama, the Folies Dramatiques, the Vaudeville, and the Gaumont Palace, then called the Hippodrome. I saw *Zigomar* and *Fantômas*, *Les Exploits de Maciste* and *Les Mystères de New York*: the gilding spoilt my pleasure. The Vaudeville, formerly a theatre, refused to yield up its old grandeur: up to the last minute, a red curtain with gold tassels hid the screen; three knocks would announce the beginning of the performance, the orchestra would play an overture, the curtain would go up and the lights out. I was annoyed by this incongruous ceremony, by the dusty pomp which achieved nothing except to remove the characters to a distance; in the circle, in the gods, impressed by the chandeliers and by the paintings on the ceiling, our fathers could not or would not believe that the theatre belonged to them: they were received there. I wanted to see the film *as close as possible*. In the egalitarian discomfort of the local halls, I had realized that this new art was mine, was everyone's. We had the same mental age: I was seven and could read; it was twelve and could not speak. They said that it was just starting and that it would improve; I thought we would grow up together. I have not forgotten our mutual childhood: when I am offered a boiled sweet, when a woman near me varnishes her nails, when I breathe a certain smell of disinfectant in the lavatories of provincial hotels or when I stare at the small violet night-light on the ceiling of a night-train, I recapture in my eyes, in my nose and on my tongue, the scents and the lights of those vanished halls; four years ago, at sea off Fingal's Cave, in heavy weather, I could hear a piano in the wind.

Inaccessible to the sacred, I adored magic: the cinema was a dubious phenomenon which I loved perversely for what it still lacked. That stream of light was everything, nothing, and everything reduced to nothing: I was present at the frenzies of a wall; solid objects had been robbed of a massiveness which bore down even on my body, and the young idealist in me delighted at this endless contraction; later on, the lateral and circular movements of triangles reminded me of those shapes

77

gliding across the screen. I loved the cinema even for its two-dimensional quality. I made primary colours of its white and black, comprising all the others and revealing themselves only to the initiate; I loved seeing the invisible. Above all, I loved the immutable dumbness of my heroes. But no: they were not mute because they knew how to make themselves understood. We communicated through music; it was the sound of what was going on inside them. Persecuted innocence did better than to speak of or show its woe: it stole its way into me through the tune which issued from it; I would read the conversations, but I understood the hope and the bitterness, and caught a whisper of the proud suffering that did not proclaim itself. I was committed: *that was not me*, that young widow crying on the screen, and yet she and I had but one soul: Chopin's *Funeral March*; that was all it needed for her tears to moisten my eyes. I felt that I was a prophet unable to foretell anything: even before the traitor was betrayed, his crime would steal its way into me; when all seemed quiet in the château, sinister chords would betray the presence of the murderer. How lucky those cowboys, musketeers and policemen were: their future was there, in that foreboding music, and it determined the present. An unbroken song mingled with their lives and led them on towards victory or death, as it moved towards its own end. They were expected, these men: by the young girl in peril, by the general, by the traitor ambushed in the forest and by the friend tethered near a barrel of powder as he sadly watched the flame run along the fuse. The course of that flame, the virgin's desperate struggle against her ravisher, the hero galloping across the steppes, the interweaving of all these images, of all these speeds and, underneath them, the hell-bent movement of the 'Race to the Abyss', an orchestral selection from *The Damnation of Faust* adapted for the piano, all meant one thing to me: Destiny. The hero would jump down, put out the fuse, the traitor would go for him, and a duel with knives would begin; but the hazards of this duel would themselves become part of the strict musical development: they were false hazards which poorly concealed the universal order. What joy when the last knife-stab coincided with the last chord!

I was satisfied, I had found the world in which I wanted to live – I was in touch with the absolute. What uneasiness, too, when the lights went on again: I was torn with love for these characters and they had disappeared, taking their world with them; I had felt their victory in my bones, yet it was theirs and not mine: out in the street, I was a supernumerary once more.

I resolved to dispense with speech and live through music. I had the opportunity every evening about five. My grandfather would be giving classes at the Institute of Modern Languages; my grandmother would have retired to her room to read Gyp*; my mother would have given me my tea, started the dinner and given the maid her final instructions; she would sit down at the piano and play Chopin's *Ballades*, a Schumann sonata, Franck's *Symphonic Variations* and sometimes, at my request, the overture to *Fingal's Cave*. I would slip into the study. It would already be getting dark in there, and two candles would be burning on the piano. Under cover of the twilight, I would seize my grandfather's ruler, my rapier, and his paper-knife, my dagger; I immediately became the double of a musketeer. Sometimes, inspiration would be slow in coming: to gain time, I, as a famous bravo, would decide that important business forced me to remain incognito. I had to take blows without returning them and screw myself up to feign cowardice. I would wander about the room, scowling, head down, dragging my feet; I would show by an occasional start that someone had slapped me or kicked my bottom, but I took care not to react; I noted down the name of the man who had insulted me. Taken in huge doses, the music would at last begin to work. Like a voodoo drum, the piano would impose its rhythm on me. The *Fantaisie Impromptu* would oust my soul, dwell in me, endow me with an unknown past, a brilliant, deadly future. I was possessed; the devil had seized me and shaken me like a plum-tree. To horse! I was both mare and rider; riding and ridden, I would cross, at top speed, moors, ploughed fields, and the study, from door to window. 'You're

* Pen-name of Sybille Gabrielle Marie Antoinette de Riqueti de Mirabeau, Comtesse de Martel de Janville (1849–1932), famous for her vivacious and witty novels.

making too much noise; the neighbours will complain,' my mother would say, still playing. I did not answer her because I was dumb. I would espy the duke, dismount, and let him know by the silent movement of my lips that I thought him a bastard. He would unleash his mercenaries and the twirls of my foil would create a wall of steel round me; from time to time I would piece a breast. Immediately, I would switch parts, become the transfixed swashbuckler, fall down and die on the carpet. Then I would steal quietly away from the corpse, stand up and resume my role of knight errant. I would impersonate all the characters; as the knight, I would strike the duke; then I would change over; as the duke, I would receive the blow. But I did not interpret the bad men for long; I was always impatient to get back to the big star role, to myself. Invincible, I triumphed over everyone. But, as in my bedtime stories, I would delay any triumph indefinitely, because I was afraid of the anticlimax to come.

I was the protector of a young countess against the king's own brother. What a blood-bath! But my mother would turn the page; the allegro would give way to a gentle adagio; I hurriedly concluded the slaughter and smiled at my protégée. She loved me; the music said so. And I loved her, too, perhaps: a loving lingering heart came to birth in me. What do you do when you love? I would take her arm and walk with her round a meadow: surely that was not enough. Hastily summoned, ruffians and mercenaries rescued me from my predicament: they would fling themselves at us, a hundred to one; I would kill ninety of them and the other ten would abduct the countess.

At this moment, years of gloom lay ahead of me: the woman who loved me was a prisoner; I had all the police in the kingdom on my heels; outlawed, hounded and wretched, I had only my conscience and my sword. I would pace the study with an air of defeat and steep myself in the passionate melancholy of Chopin. Sometimes, I would skip through my life and jump two or three years ahead to reasure myself that all would end well, that I would be given back my titles, my lands, and a betrothed almost unharmed, and that the king would ask my forgiveness. But immediately, I would leap backwards, return to reinstate myself, two or three years earlier, in misfortune. This moment I loved: fiction was mingled with truth; an unhappy wanderer in pursuit of justice, I might have been the brother of the bored child, perplexed by himself, in search of a *raison d'être*, who prowled to music about his grandfather's study. Without deserting the role, I would take advantage of the resemblance to unite our fates: confident of final victory, I saw in my trials the surest means of achieving it; through my abasement, I could perceive the glory to come which was the true cause of it. Schumann's sonata managed to convince me; I was the being in despair and the God who has saved him since the beginning of the world. What joy to be able to grieve to no purpose; I had the right to lour at the universe. Weary of too easy successes, I savoured the delights of melancholy, the bitter pleasures of resentment. Object of the most tender care, pampered and without desires, I flung myself into imaginary destitution: eight years of happiness had resulted only in giving me a taste for martyrdom. For my ordinary judges, all prejudiced in my favour, I substituted a sour-faced bench, ready to condemn me without a hearing: from it I would drag an acquittal, congratulations, and an exemplary reward. Twenty times over, I had read, passionately, the story of patient Griselda; yet I did not like to suffer and my early inclinations were cruel; the defender of so many princesses was quite happy to imagine spanking the little girl who lived across the landing. What I liked about this hardly commendable tale was the victim's sadism and that inflexible virtue which, in the end, brought the cruel husband to his knees. That was what I wanted for myself: to force the magistrates to their knees, and make them do reverence to me, as punishment. But each day I postponed the acquittal to the next: always a future hero, I longed ardently for a consecration which I was for ever thrusting away.

I think this twin melancholy, felt and acted, reflected my disappointment: my feats, laid end to end, were nothing but a string of chances; when my mother had struck the final chords of the *Fantaisie Impromptu*, I would drift back to the time immemorial of orphans with no fathers and knights-errant with no orphans; hero or schoolboy, doing and re-doing the same dictations and the same feats. I was confined as in a prison – in repetition. Yet the future existed; the cinema had revealed it to me; I dreamed of having a destiny. Griselda's sulks eventually wearied me: it was no good putting off indefinitely the historic moment of my glorification; I was not making a genuine future of it: it was merely a deferred present.

It was about this time – 1912 or 1913 – that I read *Michel Strogoff*.* I wept with joy: what a model life! This officer did not have to wait the good pleasure of brigands to show his courage: an order from above had drawn him from obscurity. He lived to obey and died in his triumph; this glory meant death: the last page of the book turned, Michel would be buried alive in his little gilt-edged coffin. No worries: he was vindicated from his first appearance. Nor the slightest risk: it was true that he was constantly on the move, but matters of importance – his courage, the vigilance of the enemy, the nature of the ground, the means of communication, and a dozen other factors, all given in advance – meant that you could, all the time, pin-point his position on the map. No repetition: everything changed, and must keep changing; his future would shed light on it, and he guided himself by a star. Three months later, I read the same novel with the same excitement. Yet I did not like Michel; I found him too good: it was his fate that I envied. What I adored in him, under cover, was the Christian they had prevented me from being. The tsar of all the Russias was God the Father; conjured from nothingness by a special decree, Michel, entrusted, like all creatures, with a unique and vital mission, passed through our vale of tears, avoiding temptations and surmounting obstacles, savouring martyrdom and enjoying supernatural aid,† glorifying his Creator and then, his task complete, entering into immortality. This book was like poison to me: so there were chosen people? Their paths were dictated by the sternest exigencies? Saintliness repelled me: in Michel Strogoff, it fascinated me because it wore the trappings of heroism.

* Novel by Jules Verne (1828–1905).
† Saved by the miracle of a tear. (*Author's footnote*.)

82

Yet I did not alter my dumb-show one bit and the idea of a mission hung in the air, an insubstantial ghost which never managed to assume flesh and of which I could never get rid. Naturally, my confederates, the kings of France, were at my orders and only waiting for a signal to give me theirs. I did not ask for any. If you risk your life through obedience, what becomes of generosity? Marcel Dunot, the iron-fisted boxer, would surprise me each week by doing, with good grace, more than his duty; blind, covered with glorious wounds, Michel Strogoff would hardly admit that he had done his. I admired his bravery, but I disapproved of his humility: this brave man had only the sky above his head; why did he bow before the tsar when it was the tsar who ought to have kissed his feet? But unless you humbled yourself, whence was to come your mandate to live? This contradiction plunged me into serious perplexity. Sometimes, I would try to sidestep the difficulty: an unnoticed child, I would hear talk of some dangerous mission; I would go and fling myself at the king's feet and beg him to entrust it to me. He would refuse: I was too young and the matter too grave. I would stand up, provoke his captains to duel with me, and beat the lot of them. The sovereign would submit to the evidence: 'Go, then, if you must!' But I would not be taken in by my trick and I was well aware that I had forced it on myself. And then these apes disgusted me: I was a *sans-culotte* and a regicide, and my grandfather had warned me against tyrants, whether they were called Louis xvi or Badinguet.* What was more, I used to read Michel Zévaco's serial story in *Le Matin* every day: this author of genius, influenced by Hugo, had invented the republican cloak-and-dagger novel. His heroes stood for the people; they created and destroyed empires, predicted the French Revolution back in the fourteenth century, protected, out of the kindness of their hearts, infant kings or mad kings against their ministers, and boxed the ears of wicked kings. The greatest of them all, Pardaillan, was my master: standing grandly on my bantam's legs, I have slapped Henri iii and Louis xiii scores of times, in imitation of him. Could I submit to their orders after that? In a word, I

* Nickname of Napoleon iii.

could neither find within myself the imperative mandate which would have justified my presence in this world nor recognize the right of anyone else to deliver it to me. Listlessly I took to horseback again and languished in the fray; absent-minded butcher or lazy martyr, I remained Griselda, for want of a tsar, a God, or, quite simply, a father.

I was leading two existences, both of them lies. In public, I was an impostor: the famous grandson of the well-known Charles Schweitzer; alone, I was absorbed by an imaginary fit of sulks. I corrected my false glory by a false incognito. I had no difficulty in switching from one role to the other: just as I was about to make my secret thrust, the key would turn in the lock, my mother's hands, suddenly paralysed, would rest motionless on the keys. I would put down the ruler in the library and go and fling myself into my grandfather's arms; I would push forward his armchair, bring him his fur-lined slippers and ask him what sort of day he had had, referring to his pupils by name. Whatever the depth of my dream, I was never in danger of losing myself in it. Yet I was threatened: my true self was in danger of remaining those alternating lies of mine to the very end.

I had another true self. Children would be playing on the terraces of the Luxembourg Gardens. I would go up to them, but they brushed past me without seeing me as I looked at them with the eyes of a beggar. How strong and fleet they were! In the presence of these flesh and blood heroes, I lost my prodigious intelligence, my universal knowledge, my athletic frame, and my ruffianly poise; I would lean against a tree, and wait. If the leader of the group had called out to me bullyingly: 'Forward, Pardaillan, you'll be the prisoner!' I would have given up my privileges. Even a non-speaking part would have satisfied me; I would gladly have agreed to be a wounded man on a stretcher, or a corpse. I was not given the opportunity: I had met my true judges: my contemporaries, my equals; and their indifference condemned me. I never got over being unmasked by them: neither a wonder nor a jelly-fish, but a shrimp that interested no one. My mother concealed her indignation badly: this tall, beautiful woman had been coming to terms admirably with my lack of height; she found it quite natural: the Schweitzers are tall and the Sartres are short; I took after my father, that was all. She was glad that, aged eight, I had remained easy to carry and manage: my small size was simply a prolongation of my early years. But, when she saw that no one asked me to play, her love made her guess that I was in danger of seeing myself as a dwarf – which I am not quite – and of suffering from it. To save me from despair, she used to feign impatience: 'What are you waiting for, you great booby? Ask them if they'll play with you.' I would shake my head. I would have agreed to the most menial of tasks but it was a point of pride not to ask for them. She would indicate some ladies who sat knitting on iron seats: 'Would you like me to speak to their mothers?' I would beg her to do nothing of the sort, she would take my hand and we would set off, going from tree to tree, from group to group, ever pleading and ever rejected. At dusk, I would be back on my perch, on the heights where my mind could breathe, among my dreams: I would avenge my discomfitures with half a dozen precocious remarks and the slaughter of a hundred mercenaries. It was no good: it did not work.

I was saved by my grandfather: he flung me, without meaning to, into a fresh imposture which changed my life.

PART TWO

*

WRITING

CHARLES SCHWEITZER had never thought of himself as a writer, but the French language still amazed him, at the age of seventy, because he had learnt it with difficulty and had not quite made it his own: he used to play with it, he enjoyed the words and liked saying them, and his merciless diction did not spare one syllable; when he had time, his pen would sort them out into bunches. He would readily illustrate what happened in our family and at the University by works improvised for the occasion: New Year and birthday greetings, compliments at wedding breakfasts, speeches in verse for St Charlemagne's day,* playlets, charades, verses to set rhymes, and kindly commonplaces; at conferences, he would improvise quatrains, in German and in French.

In early summer, the two women and myself would leave for Arcachon, before my grandfather had finished his classes. He used to write to us three times a week: two pages for Louise, a postscript for Anne-Marie, and a whole letter in verse for myself. To make me savour my good fortune still more, my mother learnt and taught me the rules of versification. Someone caught me scribbling a reply in verse, encouraged me to complete it, and helped me with it. When the two women sent the letter, they laughed till they cried as they imagined the recipient's astonishment. I received a poem in my praise by return of post; I replied with a poem. The habit was formed; the grandfather and his grandson were bound by a new link; they talked, like Indians or the pimps of Montmartre, in a language forbidden to women. I was given a rhyming dictionary, and made myself a versifier: I used to write madrigals for Vévé, a little fair-haired girl confined to a couch who was to die a few years

* Festival celebrated by schoolboys on 28 January in honour of Charlemagne, founder of schools. He was canonized by the anti-pope Pascal III in 1165, a canonization that has never been either ratified or denounced.

later. The little girl did not give a damn for them: she was an angel; but the admiration of a large audience consoled me for her indifference. I have come across some of those poems again. All children have genius, except Minou Drouet, said Cocteau in 1955. In 1912, they all had it except me: I wrote imitatively, formally, pretending to be grown-up: I wrote mainly because I was Charles Schweitzer's grandson. I was given La Fontaine's *Fables*; they displeased me: the author had taken things easily. I decided to rewrite them in alexandrines. The undertaking was beyond me and I got the impression that it made people smile: that was my last poetic experiment. But I was launched: I switched from verse to prose and had not the slightest trouble re-inventing in writing the thrilling adventures which I read in *Cri-Cri*. It was about time: I was to discover the futility of my dreams. Through my flights of imagination, I was trying to attain reality. When my mother asked me, without looking away from her music: 'Poulou, what are you doing?' I would sometimes break my vow of silence and answer: 'I'm making films.' In fact, I was trying to tear ideas from my mind and bring them to life outside myself, amidst real furniture and real walls, as bright and clear as the ones which flowed on the screen. In vain; I could no longer ignore my twofold imposture: I was pretending to be an actor pretending to be a hero.

I had no sooner begun to write than I laid down my pen to exult. The imposture was the same but I have explained that I saw words as the quintessence of things. Nothing disturbed me more than to see my scrawl little by little exchange its will-o'-the-wisp sheen for the dull consistency of matter: it was the imaginary made real. Trapped in their names, a lion, a Second Empire captain, a Bedouin were introduced into the dining-room; they remained there for ever imprisoned, given body by signs; it was as if I had anchored my dreams to the world by the scratching of a steel nib. I asked for an exercise-book and a bottle of violet ink, and wrote on the cover: 'Exercise-book for novels.' I called the first one I completed *Pour un papillon* (for a butterfly). A professor, his daughter, and a young, athletic explorer were going up the Amazon in search of a precious butterfly. I had borrowed the plot, the characters, the details of their adventures, even the title from a story in pictures which had appeared during the previous term. This deliberate plagiarism released me from my final qualms: it must all be true because I had invented none of it. I had no ambition to be published but I had arranged it so that I was printed in advance and I did not set down a line that was not to be found in my model. Did I see myself as a plagiarist? No. As an original writer: I touched up and renovated; for instance, I had taken care to change the names of the characters. These minor alterations enabled me to blend memory and imagination. New and complete sentences formed in my head with the unwavering certainty attributed to inspiration. I transcribed them and, before my very eyes, they acquired the solidity of objects. If, as is commonly held, an inspired author is, deep down, something other than himself, I knew inspiration between the ages of seven and eight.

I was never quite taken in by this 'automatic writing'. But I enjoyed the game for its own sake: an only son, I could play it alone. Now and then, I used to stop writing and pretend to hesitate so that I could feel I was, with my furrowed brow and far-away look, *a writer*. Besides, I adored plagiarism, through snobbery, and I deliberately carried it to extremes, as will be seen.

Boussenard and Jules Verne did not lose any opportunity of tutoring me: at moments of crisis, they would break off the flow of the story to plunge into a description of some poisonous plant or some native locality. As a reader, I skipped these didactic passages; as a writer, I crammed my novels with them. I aspired to teach my contemporaries all that I did not know: the customs of the inhabitants of Tierra del Fuego, African flora, the climate of the desert. Separated by a blow of fate, then boarding, without realizing it, the same ship, and victims of the same shipwreck, the butterfly-collector and his daughter would be clinging to the same buoy; they would look up and call out in turn: 'Daisy!' 'Father!' Alas, a dog-fish would be on the prowl in search of fresh meat and it would draw near, its belly gleaming in the waves. Would the unfortunate wretches escape death? I would go and fetch volume Pr-Z of the *Grand Larousse*, carry it with difficulty over to my desk, open it at the right page, and copy it out word for word when I came to the line: 'Sharks are common in the tropical Atlantic. These large and most voracious salt-water fish may be as much as forty feet long and weigh up to eight tons. . . .' I would take my time transcribing the entry: I felt I was deliciously boring, as distinguished as Boussenard, and, since I had not yet worked out how to save my heroes, I would shiver with exquisite terror.

Everything conspired to make this new activity just one more monkey-trick. My mother showered me with encouragement and brought visitors into the dining-room to surprise the young creator at his school-desk; I would pretend to be too absorbed to notice my admirers; they would steal out murmuring how very sweet, how very charming I was. My uncle Émile made me a present of a small typewriter which I did not use. Madame Picard bought me a hemispherical map of the world so that I could plot my globe-trotters' route without fear of error. Anne-Marie copied out my second novel, *Le Marchand de bananes* (the banana merchant), on smooth paper, and it was handed round. Even Mamie encouraged me: 'At least he's being good,' she said, 'he's not making a noise.' Fortunately, my dedication was postponed by my grandfather's disapproval.

Karl had never endorsed what he called my 'trashy reading'. When my mother informed him that I had begun to write, he was at first delighted, hoping, I suppose, for some account of the family, with piquant observations and adorable artlessness. He picked up my exercise-book, turned the pages, made a face, and left the dining-room, disgusted to find, from my pen, the same 'rubbish' as in my favourite magazines. He took no further interest in my work. Mortified, my mother tried several times to catch him by surprise and make him read *Le Marchand de bananes*. She would wait for him to put on his slippers and sit in his armchair; while he was resting in silence, his eyes fixed coldly on nothing, his hands on his knees, she would take up my manuscript, turn the pages idly and then, suddenly enraptured, would start laughing to herself. In the end, irresistibly carried away, she would hand it to my grandfather: 'Read that, Papa. It's *too* amusing.' But he would thrust aside the notebook or, if he glanced at it, it was to point out ill-humouredly my spelling mistakes. In the end, my mother became intimidated: not daring to congratulate me and afraid to hurt me, she stopped reading what I wrote so that she need not talk to me about it.

Barely tolerated, passed over in silence, my literary activities relapsed into half-secrecy; yet I pursued them assiduously: during my free time, on Thursdays and on Sundays, in the holidays, and, when I was lucky enough to be ill, in bed; I remember some pleasant convalescent periods and a black exercise-book with red-edged pages which I took up and put down like a piece of tapestry. I made fewer films: my novels took the place of everything else. In short, I wrote for my own pleasure.

My plots became more complex; I introduced a wide variety of incident, pouring everything I read, good and bad, haphazardly into these hold-alls. The stories suffered; yet there was a gain: I had to invent linking passages and I immediately became a little less of a plagiarist. And then I divided myself in half. The previous year, when I was 'making films', I was acting myself, flinging myself whole-heartedly into the world of imagination, and convinced more than once that I was completely engulfed in it. As an author, I was still the hero: I projected my epic dreams through him. Yet there were two of us: he did not bear my name and I referred to him only in the third person. Instead of endowing him with gestures, I fashioned for him, in words, a body which I pretended I could see. This sudden 'standing aloof' might have frightened me: it delighted me; I was happy to be *he* without his being entirely me. He was my puppet, I could bend him to my whims, put him to the test, pierce his side with a lance and then look after him as my mother looked after me, cure him as she cured me. My favourite authors, out of a residue of shame, stopped half-way along the road to sublimity: even in Zévaco's novels no hero ever defeated more than twenty sturdy ruffians at a time. I wanted to revolutionize the adventure story, so I threw credibility overboard, and multiplied both enemies and dangers: to save his future father-in-law and his betrothed the young explorer in *Pour un papillon* struggled three days and three nights against

93

the sharks; in the end the sea was red; the same man, wounded, escaped from a ranch besieged by Apaches, crossed the desert clutching his guts, and refused to be stitched up until he had spoken to the general. A little later, under the name of Götz von Berlichingen,* the very same man put an army to rout. One against all: that was my rule; the source of this gloomy but grandiose dream is to be found in the bourgeois and puritan individualism of those around me.

A hero, I struggled against tyrannies; as a Demiurge, I became a tyrant myself and was familiar with all the temptations of power. I was harmless but I became wicked. Who was to stop me from putting out Daisy's eyes? Half dead with fear, I told myself: nothing. And I put them out as I would have torn the wings off a fly. I wrote, my heart pounding: 'Daisy passed her hand before her eyes: she had gone blind' and I remained startled, pen in air: I had produced in the absolute a trivial incident which compromised me delightfully. I was not really sadistic: my perverse delight would suddenly turn to panic, I would annul all my decrees, covering them with crossings-out to make them illegible: the young girl would recover her sight or, rather, she had never lost it. But the memory of my whims tortured me a long while: I gave myself cause for great worry.

The world of fiction worried me, too: sometimes, weary of gentle massacres fit for children, I let myself go, and I discovered, in the anguish of hideous possibility, a monstrous universe which was merely the reverse side of my omnipotence. I thought: anything can happen! and this meant: I can imagine anything. Trembling, continually about to tear up my sheet of paper, I described supernatural horrors. If my mother happened to read over my shoulder, she would give a cry of triumph and alarm: 'What imagination!' She would bite her lip, try to speak, find nothing to say and run away abruptly: her confusion set the seal on my anguish. But it was nothing to do with imagination: I did not invent these horrors; I discovered them, like everything else, in my memory.

During this period, the West was dying of suffocation: it was what was called 'soft living'. Since it had no visible enemies,

* Hero of an early play by Goethe.

94

the bourgeoisie enjoyed being scared of its own shadow; it bartered its boredom for a tempered anxiety. There was talk of spiritualism and of ectoplasm. At No. 2 rue le Goff, opposite our block, table-turning was practised. This took place on the fourth floor: 'at the wise man's', my grandmother used to say. Sometimes she would call us and we would come in time to see several pairs of hands on a pedestal table, but someone would move across to the window and draw the curtains. Louise made out that every day the wise man received children of my own age, brought by their mothers. 'And,' she used to say, 'I can see him: he gives them the laying-on of hands.' My grandfather would shake his head but, although he condemned these practices, he did not dare to ridicule them. My mother was frightened of them, while my grandmother, for once, appeared more intrigued than sceptical. In the end, they agreed: 'You don't want to meddle in it, it unhinges you!' There was a craze for fantastic stories; respectable newspapers supplied two or three a week to the dechristianized public which missed the elegances of faith. The narrator would recount, with complete objectivity, some disturbing fact; but he left a loophole for positivism: however strange, the event might have a rational explanation. The author would search for the explanation, find it, and loyally serve it up to us. But, almost immediately, he would deploy his skill to show us how inadequate and frivolous it was. That was all: the story would end with a question-mark. But it was enough: the Other World was there, the more to be feared because it was not mentioned.

Whenever I opened *Le Matin*, I was chilled with terror. One story in particular struck me. I still remember its title: *Du vent dans les arbres* (wind in the trees). One summer evening, a sick woman, alone on the first floor of her country house, was tossing and turning in her bed; a chestnut-tree thrust its branches through the open window into the room. On the ground floor, several people had gathered; they were chatting and watching night descend on the garden. Suddenly one of them pointed to the chestnut-tree: 'Look, look! Is there some wind, then?' They were astonished and went out on the steps: not a breath of wind; yet the leaves were rustling. At that moment, a cry! the sick woman's husband dashed up the stairs and found his young bride upright in bed: she pointed at the tree and fell back dead; the chestnut-tree had reassumed its normal stillness. What had she seen? A madman had escaped from the asylum: he must have been hiding in the tree and have shown his grinning face. It was he, it *must* have been he, for the simple reason that no other explanation would do. And yet. . . . How was it they had not seen him climb up it? Or come down? How was it the dogs had not barked? How was it that he had been arrested, six hours later, more than sixty miles away from the property? Questions without an answer. The story-teller dodged the issue and casually summed up: 'If the villagers are to be believed, it was Death that shook the branches of the chestnut-tree.' I threw away the newspaper, stamped my foot and shouted: 'No! No!' My heart was pounding fit to burst. One day, in the train from Limoges, I thought I should faint, as I was turning the pages of the Hachette almanac: I came across a hair-raising illustration: a moonlit quay, a long rugged claw emerged from the water, grabbed a drunkard, and dragged him down to the bottom of the dock. The picture illustrated a text which I read avidly and which ended – approximately – with these words: 'Was it a drunkard's hallucination? Had Hell gaped?' I was afraid of water, of crabs, and of trees. Above all, I was afraid of books: I cursed the tormentors who peopled their stories with these loathsome shapes. Yet I imitated them.

Of course, it had to be the right moment. For instance, at dusk: shadows would be filling the dining-room. I would push my little desk over to the window, my anguish would return, and the docility of my heroes, unfailingly sublime, misunderstood and vindicated, would betray their lack of substance; then *it* would come: an invisible, bewildering creature would hypnotize me; in order to see it you had to describe it. I would quickly end my current adventure, remove my characters to another region of the globe – usually under the sea or underground – and hastily expose them to fresh dangers: changed on the spur of the moment into divers or geologists, they would discover the Creature's tracks, follow them and, all of a sudden, meet it. What then issued from my pen – an octopus with fiery eyes, a twenty-ton crustacean, or a giant talking-spider – was myself, a childish monster; it was my boredom with life, my fear of death, my mawkishness and my perversity. I did not recognize myself: as soon as it was engendered, the loathsome creature would turn on me and on my courageous potholers; I would fear for their lives, my heart would give a leap, I would forget my hand tracing out the words and would think I was reading them. Very often, it stopped there; I did not yield the men up to the Beast nor did I get them out of trouble; in short, it was enough that I had brought them together. I would get up and go to the kitchen or the library; the next day, I would leave one or two pages blank and launch my characters off on some new exploit. Strange 'novels', always unfinished, always picked up again or continued, whichever you like, under other titles, a hotch-potch of grim tales and carefree adventures, fantastic incidents and extracts from the encyclopedia. I have lost them and I sometimes think it is a pity: if I had thought of putting them under lock and key, they would bring back to me my whole childhood.

I began to discover myself. I was virtually nothing, at most an activity without any content, but that was enough. I was escaping from the Comedy: I was not yet working but I had already stopped playing; the liar was finding his true self in elaborating his lies. I was born from writing: before that, there was only a reflection in a mirror. From my first novel, I knew that a child had entered the palace of mirrors. By writing, I existed, I escaped from the grown-ups; but I existed only to write and if I said: me – that meant the me who wrote. It did not matter: I knew joy; the public child gave himself private assignations.

It was too good to last: I should have remained sincere if I had preserved my secrecy; it was torn from me. I was coming to the age at which it is agreed that middle-class children should reveal the first signs of their vocation. We had been told for a long time that my Schweitzer cousins at Guérigny would be engineers like their father: there was not a moment to lose. Madame Picard wanted to be the first to discover the mark that

97

I carried on my forehead. 'This child will write!' she said with conviction. Annoyed, Louise gave her little tight smile; Blanche Picard turned to her and repeated sternly: 'He will write! He was born to write.' My mother knew that Charles barely encouraged me: she was afraid of complications and she looked at me with her short-sighted eyes. 'Do you think so, Blanche? Do you think so?' But in the evening, when I leapt on to my bed, in my nightshirt, she gave my shoulders a hard squeeze and said with a smile: 'My little fellow will write!' My grandfather was tactfully informed: they feared an explosion. He merely shook his head and I heard him confide to Monsieur Simonnot, the following Thursday, that no one, in the autumn of his life, could witness the birth of a talent without being moved. He continued to ignore my scribblings but, when his German pupils came to the house for dinner, he would lay his hand on my skull and would say, isolating each syllable so as not to lose an opportunity of teaching them French phrases by the direct method: 'He's got the bump of literature.'

He did not believe a word he was saying, but what of that? The harm was done; it might get worse if I was met head on: I would perhaps grow stubborn. Karl announced my vocation so as to preserve a chance of steering me away from it. He was the opposite of a cynic, but he was getting old: his enthusiasms wearied him; deep down in his thoughts, in a cold and seldom-visited desert, I was sure that *he* knew what was what about me, the family and himself. One day, while I was reading, lying between his feet, in the middle of one of those interminable stony silences which he imposed on the family, an idea crossed his mind and made him forget my presence. He looked at my mother reproachfully: 'And supposing he got it into his head to live by the pen?' My grandfather enjoyed Verlaine and he owned a selection of his poetry. But he thought that he had seen him, in 1894, 'drunk as a pig', enter a pub in the rue Saint-Jacques: this meeting had confirmed him in his contempt for professional writers, ludicrous miracle-mongers who asked for a golden louis to show you the moon and, in the end, showed you their backsides for a hundred sous. My mother looked startled but did not reply: she knew that Charles held other views about me. In most of the *lycées*, the teacher of German was an Alsatian who had opted for France and whose patriotism it was desired to reward: trapped between two nations, two languages, these Alsatians had had their studies broken, and there were gaps in their culture; they suffered from it; they also complained that the hostility of their colleagues isolated them from the teaching community. I would be their avenger, I would avenge my grandfather. Though the grandson of an Alsatian, I was, at the same time, a Frenchman of France; Karl would see to it that I acquired universal knowledge, and I would take the royal road: in my person, martyred Alsace would enter the École Normale Supérieure, take a degree brilliantly and become a prince: a teacher of literature. One evening, he told me that he wanted to talk to me man to man; the women withdrew, he took me on his knee and talked to me solemnly. I would write, that was understood; I must know him well enough to have no fear that he would stand in the way of my wishes. But I had to see things as they were, clearly. A man could not live by literature. Did I know that famous writers had died of hunger? That others had sold themselves in order to eat? If I wished to keep my independence, it was advisable to choose a second calling. Being a teacher gave you leisure; the preoccupations of academic men were similar to those of writers: I would be constantly passing from one priesthood to the other; I should be constantly in touch with great authors; at one and the same time I should disclose their works to my pupils and derive my inspiration from them. I could forget my provincial loneliness in the composition of poems or in translating Horace into blank verse. I could contribute short literary articles to the local papers, a brilliant essay on the teaching of Greek and another on adolescent psychology to the *Revue pédagogique*. At my death, unpublished works would be found in my drawers: a meditation on the sea, a one-act play, and a few erudite, sensitive pages on the monuments of Aurillac, enough for a slim volume which would be published through the efforts of my former pupils.

For some time, whenever my grandfather went into raptures over my virtues, I had remained cold; I still pretended to listen to the voice which trembled with love when it called me 'a present from Heaven' but in the end I had stopped hearing it. Why did I pay attention to it that very day when it was telling the most deliberate lies? Through what misunderstanding had I made it say the opposite of what it claimed to tell me? It was the voice that had changed: it was dry and hard, and I took it for that of the absentee who had begotten me. Charles had two faces: when he was acting the grandfather, I treated him as a clown of my own kind and had no respect for him. But if he spoke to Monsieur Simonnot, to his sons, or when, while he was being served by his women at table, he pointed without a word to the cruet or the bread-basket, I admired his authority. The way he made use of his forefinger, in particular, impressed me: he was careful not to extend it; he moved it vaguely in the air, half-crooked, so that you could not be sure where he was pointing and the two women who waited on him had to guess his orders; sometimes, in her exasperation, my grandmother would make a mistake and pass him the fruit-dish when he wanted a drink: I blamed my grandmother and bowed before these regal desires which should have been anticipated rather than fulfilled. If Charles had called out from a long way off, spreading his arms: 'Here's the new Hugo, here's the budding Shakespeare!' I should today be an industrial designer or a professor of literature. He carefully avoided it: for the first time I had dealings with the patriarch; he seemed morose and the more venerable because he had forgotten how to adore me. It was Moses dictating the new law. My law. He had mentioned my vocation only to emphasize its disadvantages: I assumed that he took it as settled. If he had predicted that I should soak my paper with my tears or that I should roll on the carpet, my middle-class restraint would have taken fright. He convinced me of my vocation by making me realize that such ostentatious displays were not for me: to deal with Aurillac or the teaching profession, there was no need, alas, for frenzies or upheavals; others would take it upon themselves to shed the immortal tears of the twentieth century. I resigned myself to the absence of lightning, to shining in literature through domestic qualities, through my graciousness and my diligence.

The writing profession seemed to me a grown-up activity, so heavily serious, so pointless and, deep down, so without interest that I did not doubt for a second that it was to be mine. I thought at the time: 'That's all there is to it' and 'I'm gifted'. Like all dreamers, I mistook disenchantment for truth.

Karl had turned me inside out like a rabbit-skin: I had thought I was writing only to set down my dreams when, according to him, I dreamed only to exercise my pen. My torments, my imaginary passions were simply my talent's ruses; they had no other function than to lead me day by day to my desk and supply me with narrative themes suitable to my age while I waited for the great themes that would come with experience and maturity. I lost my mythical illusions: 'Ah!' said my grandmother, 'it's not just a question of having eyes, you have to learn how to use them. Do you know what Flaubert did to the young Maupassant? He sat him down in front of a tree and gave him two hours to describe it.' So I learned to look. Preordained bard of the buildings of Aurillac, I gazed mournfully at those other monuments: the blotter, the piano, and the clock which would also – why not? – be immortalized by my future impositions. I observed. It was a depressing, disillusioning game: you had to settle yourself in front of an armchair covered with stamped velvet and inspect it. What was there to say about it? Well, that it was covered in a scratchy green material, that it had two arms, four feet, and a back on top of which were two small wooden fir-cones. That was all for the moment, but I would come back to it, I would do better next time; in the end I would know it like the palm of my hand. Later on, I would describe it and my readers would say: 'How well observed, how well seen it is, how true! Those are details you can't invent!' Painting real objects with real words traced with a real pen would have been devilish if I had not been becoming real myself too. In short, I knew, once and for all, what I had to reply to the ticket-inspectors who asked me for my ticket.

You may well believe that I appreciated my good fortune! The trouble was that I did not enjoy it. I was appointed, I was fortunate enough to have been provided with a future, and I said that it was wonderful but, on the quiet, I loathed it. Had

I asked for this scribe's burden? My dealings with great men had convinced me that you could not be a writer without becoming famous; but, when I compared the glory which was due to me with the few short treatises I was to leave behind me, I felt mystified: could I truthfully believe that my great-nephews would still read me and that they would grow enthusiastic over such a slim body of work, about subjects which already bored me? I imagined sometimes that I would be rescued from oblivion by my 'style', that enigmatic virtue which my grandfather denied to Stendhal and recognized in Renan: but these meaningless words did not succeed in reassuring me.

Above all, I had to renounce myself. Two months earlier, I had been a bravo and an athlete: that was all over! I was called upon to choose between Corneille and Pardaillan. I thrust aside Pardaillan whom I loved with a genuine love; I opted for Corneille out of humility. I had seen heroes running and fighting in the Luxembourg Gardens; dumbfounded by their beauty, I had realized that I belonged to an inferior race. I had to proclaim it, sheathe my sword in its scabbard, rejoin the common herd, and renew acquaintance with the great writers, those little squirts who did not frighten me. They had been rickety children: in that at least I was like them; they had become sickly adults, old men with catarrh, and I would be like them in that. A nobleman had had Voltaire thrashed and I should perhaps be flogged by a captain, once a swaggerer in the public gardens.

I believed myself gifted through resignation: in Charles Schweitzer's study, among the worn-out, broken-backed, incomplete books, talent was the least valued thing in the world. In the same way, under the *Ancien Régime*, many younger sons, destined from birth for the priesthood, were condemned to command battalions. One image summed up, for a long while, in my eyes, the grim pomps of notoriety: on a long table covered with a white cloth were decanters of orangeade and bottles of sparkling wine; I took a goblet and men in evening dress – there were at least fifteen of them – stood round me drinking my health. Behind us I could sense the vast and dusty immensity of a hired hall. It is clear that I expected nothing from life except that it should revive in later years, on my account, the annual gathering at the Institute of Modern Languages.

Thus was my fate determined at Number One rue le Goff, in a fifth-floor flat, below Goethe and Schiller, above Molière, Racine, and La Fontaine, and facing Heinrich Heine and Victor Hugo, amidst continually interrupted conversations. Karl and I chased out the women, embraced closely, and whispered our muted dialogues to each other, every word of which left its mark on me. With well placed little touches, Charles persuaded me that I was not a genius. In fact, I knew I was not, and I did not care; absent and impossible, heroism was the sole object of my desire: it is the blaze that warms feeble souls. My inner misery and my sense of gratuitousness forbad me to give it up altogether. I no longer dared to bewitch myself with my future actions, but deep down I was terrified: someone must have been mistaken about either the child or the vocation. Lost, I accepted in obedience to Karl, the dedicated career of a minor writer. In short, he flung me into literature by the pains he took to steer me away from it: to the extent that sometimes, even today, when I am in a bad mood, I ask myself if I have not used up so many days and nights, covered so many sheets of paper with my ink, dumped on to the market so many books that no one wanted, in the sole and mad hope of pleasing my grandfather. That would be a joke: at over fifty, to find myself embarked, in order to fulfil the wishes of a man long since dead, on an undertaking of which he would certainly have disapproved.

In fact, I am like Swann cured of his love and sighing: 'To think that I've spoiled my life for a woman who wasn't my type!' Sometimes, I am a cad in private; it is a crude health precaution. Now the cad is always right but only up to a certain point. It is true that I have no gift for writing; I have been told so, and I have been treated as good at book learning: I am; my books reek of sweat and effort, and I grant that, in the noses of our aristocrats, they stink; I have often written them against myself, in other words against everyone,* with a mental

* Be self-satisfied, and other self-satisfied people will love you, rend your neighbour, the other neighbours will laugh. But if you hurt your own soul, all other souls will cry out. (*Author's footnote.*)

exertion which has, in the end, become high blood-pressure. My commandments have been sewn into my skin: if I go a day without writing, the scar burns me; and if I write too easily, it also burns me. Today this worn exigency strikes me as clumsy and inflexible: like those solemn, prehistoric crabs which the sea washes up on the beaches of Long Island; like them, it survives from times past. I have long envied the *concierges* in the rue Lacépède, when the long summer evenings bring them out on to the pavement, astride their chairs: their innocent eyes see without feeling obliged to look.

Except for one thing: apart from a few old men who dip their pens in eau-de-Cologne and a few dandies who write like butchers, good translators do not exist. This is because of the nature of the Word: you talk in your own language, but you write in a foreign one. From this I conclude that we are all the same in our calling: all convicts, all branded. And besides, the reader has grasped that I loathe my childhood and all that remains of it: I would not listen to my grandfather's voice, that mechanical voice which wakes me with a start and impels me to my table, if it were not mine and if, between the ages of eight and ten, I had not arrogantly taken on the so-called imperative mandate which I had accepted in all humility.

> *Je sais fort bien que je ne suis qu'une*
> *machine à faire des livres.**
> (Chateaubriand)

I nearly threw in my hand. Deep down, I saw the gift which Karl half-heartedly recognized in me, judging it unwise to deny it altogether, as a mere accident, unable to justify that other accident, myself. My mother had a fine voice, *therefore* she sang. She was travelling none the less without a ticket. I had the bump of literature, therefore I would write and I would exploit this vein all my life. Agreed. But Art was losing – at least for me – its sacred powers and I should remain a vagrant – slightly better provided for, that was all. For me to feel necessary, I would have had to be clamoured for. My family had sustained me a long while in that illusion; I had been told over

* I know very well that I am only a machine for making books.

and over again that I was a gift from Heaven, much longed for, indispensable to my grandfather and to my mother. I no longer believed this, but I still felt that you were born superfluous unless sent into the world to satisfy some particular expectation. My pride and my friendlessness were such, at that time, that I wanted either to be dead or sought after by the whole world.

I stopped writing: Madame Picard's announcements had lent such importance to my written soliloquies that I no longer dared to continue them. When I wanted to take up my novel, even if only to save the young couple I had abandoned with neither provisions nor sun-helmets in the very heart of the Sahara, I felt the pangs of helplessness. I would no sooner sit down than my head would fill with fog. I chewed my nails as I made faces: I had lost my innocence. I would get up and prowl round the flat like a fire-raiser; unfortunately, I never set light to it: docile by condition, taste, and habit, I turned rebel later only through having pushed submissiveness to the extreme. I was bought 'an exercise book for duties', bound in black cloth and edged in red: no other outward sign distinguished it from my 'exercise-book for novels': as soon as I looked at it, my school tasks and my private obligations fused. I identified the author with the pupil, the pupil with the teacher-to-be; writing and teaching grammar were all one; my pen, pooled, fell from my hand and it was several months before I took it up again. My grandfather smiled in his beard when I carried my sulks to his study: he was no doubt telling himself that his shrewdness was bearing its first fruits.

It failed because I had an epic cast of mind. My sword broken, reduced to the common herd, I often had this anxiety dream at night: I was in the Luxembourg Gardens, near the pond, opposite the Senate; I had to protect, from some unknown danger, a little girl with fair hair like Vévé, who had died a year earlier. The little girl, calm and trusting, would look up at me out of her serious eyes; often, she would be holding a hoop. I was the one who was scared: I was afraid of abandoning her to invisible forces. Yet how I loved her, and with how despairing a love! I still love her; I have sought her, lost her, found her again, held her in my arms and again lost her: this is the Epic. At the age of eight, as I was becoming resigned, I gave a violent start; to save this little dead girl, I embarked on a simple but insane operation which altered the course of my life: I unloaded on to the writer the consecrated powers of the hero.

At its very start, there had been a discovery or rather a reminiscence – because, two years earlier, I had had a presentiment of it: great authors are akin to knights-errant in that both arouse passionate displays of gratitude. So far as Pardaillan was concerned, no further proof was needed: the tears of grateful orphans had furrowed the back of his hand. But, if I could believe the *Grand Larousse* and the obituary notices which I read in the papers, the writer was no less favoured: provided he lived a long while, he invariably ended by receiving a letter from a stranger *thanking* him; from then on, the thanks would never cease; they would pile up on his desk and choke his flat; foreigners would cross the seas to pay homage to him; his countrymen, after his death, would subscribe to build him a monument; in his native town, and sometimes in the capital of his country, streets would be called after him. These tokens of appreciation did not, in themselves, interest me: they reminded me too much of the family comedy. One illustration, however, bowled me over: Dickens, the famous novelist, was to land in New York in a few hours' time and the ship carrying him could be seen in the distance; the crowd, so dense that children were suffocating, was massed on the quay to greet him with open mouths and waving a thousand caps; it was lonely, widowed, orphaned, and depopulated simply by the absence of the man it was expecting. I murmured: 'There's someone lacking: it's Dickens!' and the tears sprang to my eyes. Yet I thrust aside these effects and went straight to their cause: to be so wildly acclaimed, men of letters, I thought, must have to tackle the worst of dangers and render the most distinguished services to humanity. Once in my life I had been present at a similar outburst of enthusiasm: hats flew in the air, and men and women shouted: 'Bravo! Hurrah!' It was the 14th of July and native Algerian riflemen were marching past. This memory succeeded in convincing me: in spite of their physical blemishes, their affectations and their apparent womanishness, my colleagues were a sort of soldier; they risked their lives as snipers in mysterious engagements and their military courage was applauded still more than their talent. So it is true! I thought. *They are needed!* Paris, New York, Moscow, are waiting for them, with anguish or with ecstasy, before they have published their first book, before they have begun to write – even before they are born.

But then . . . how about me? I, whose mission it was to write? Well, I was awaited. I transformed Corneille into Pardaillan: he preserved his crooked legs, his narrow chest and his emaciated face but I rid him of his avarice and his love of gain; deliberately I blended the art of writing with generosity. After that, it was child's play to change myself into Corneille and to give myself this mandate: to protect the human race. My new imposture had an odd future in store for me; meantime, I profited by it. Born unsatisfactorily, I have described my efforts to be reborn: a thousand times the prayers of innocence in peril had aroused me. But it was a joke: a false knight, I performed false deeds whose lack of substance had disgusted me in the end. Now I was being given back my dreams and they were being realized. My vocation was real; I could not doubt it because the high priest vouched for it. An imaginary child, I was becoming a real knight errant whose exploits would be real books. I was sought after! People were waiting for my works of which the first volume, in spite of my zeal, did not appear until 1935. Round about 1930, people began to get impatient and to say to each other: 'He's taking his time! We've been feeding him for twenty-five years and he's done nothing! Shall we die without reading him?' I answered them in my 1913 voice: 'Hey, give me time to work!' But pleasantly: I could see that they needed – God alone knew why – my help, and that this need had created me, myself, the one and only means of satisfying it. I strove to catch, deep down inside me, that universal expectation, my life source and my *raison d'être*; I sometimes thought that I was about to succeed and then, after a moment, I would let the whole thing go. It did not matter: these false inspirations were enough for me. Reassured, I looked outwards: perhaps in some places I was already lacking. But no: it was too early. Cherished object of a desire still unaware of itself, I joyfully continued to remain incognito for a while. Sometimes my grandmother would take me along to her lending-library and it amused me to watch tall, thoughtful, unsatisfied women glide from one wall to another in search of the author who would satisfy them; he was not to be found because it was I, that child round their skirts, at whom they did not even glance.

I laughed out of malice but I wept for pity: I had spent my short life inventing for myself tastes and prejudices which immediately became watered down. But now I had been sounded and the lead had touched rock; I was a writer just as Charles Schweitzer was a grandfather: by birth and for ever. Yet it so happened that my enthusiasm was sapped by a qualm: I refused to see an accident in the talent for which I thought Karl had vouched and I set about making a mandate of it, but, lacking encouragement and genuine demand, I could not forget that I was bestowing it on myself. Emerging from an antediluvian world, just as I was escaping from Nature to become at last myself, that Other which I aspired to be in the eyes of others, I looked my Destiny in the eyes and recognized it: it was merely my freedom, conjured up before me by my own efforts as an external force. In short, I had not quite managed to find my niche. Or entirely to disillusion myself. I was wavering. My hesitations revived an old problem: how to link the certainties of Michel Strogoff with the generosity of Pardaillan? As a knight, I had never taken orders from the king; must I agree to be an author by command? The uneasiness never lasted very long; I was the prey of two opposing mystical theologies, but I adapted myself very well to their contradictions. It even suited me to be, simultaneously, a gift from Heaven and the child of my works. When I was in a good mood, everything came from myself; I had dragged myself from nothingness by my own strength to bring men the books they needed: an obedient child, I would obey until I died, but I would obey myself. When I was depressed and aware of the sickening feebleness of my availability, I was able to soothe myself only by forcing it on predestination: I called on the human race and loaded it with responsibility for my life; I was merely the product of a collective demand. Most of the time, I achieved peace of mind by taking care never to exclude altogether either the freedom which exalts or the necessity which justifies.

Pardaillan and Strogoff were able to hit it off: the danger lay elsewhere and I was made to witness a disagreeable confrontation which forced me, afterwards, to take precautions. The chief culprit was Zévaco whom I did not distrust; was he trying to annoy me or warn me? The fact is that, one fine day, in Madrid, in a *posada*, when my one concern was for Pardaillan who was resting, poor fellow, and drinking a hard-earned glass of wine, this author drew my attention to a customer who was none other than Cervantes. The two men made friends, discovered a mutual liking, and decided to attempt a righteous surprise attack together. Worse still, Cervantes, very happy, confided to his new friend that he wanted to write a book: until then, the leading character had remained blurred but, thanks be to God, Pardaillan had appeared and would serve him as model. I was seized with indignation and almost threw the book away: what lack of tact! I was a writer-knight, I was being cut in two, and each half was becoming a whole man, meeting the other and questioning his existence. Pardaillan was no fool but he would never have written *Don Quixote*: Cervantes fought well but you could not count on him to put twenty mercenaries to flight all on his own. Their friendship itself underlined their limitations. The first thought: 'He's a bit sickly, the conceited pedant, but he's no coward.' And the second: 'By Jove, that man doesn't reason badly for a tough old soldier!' And then I was not at all pleased that my hero should serve as model for the Knight of the Sorrowful Countenance. In my 'film-making' period, I had been given a bowdlerized *Don Quixote*; but I had not read more than fifty pages of it: my exploits were being ridiculed in public! And now Zévaco himself. . . . Who was to be trusted? In reality, I was a wanton, a soldier's slut: my heart, my coward heart, preferred the adventurer to the intellectual; I was ashamed of being merely

Cervantes. To stop myself from being a traitor, I let terror reign in my mind and in my vocabulary, harried the word heroism and its substitutes, repressed the knights errant, talked to myself endlessly about men of letters, the dangers they ran and their sharp pens which skewered the wicked. I went on with my reading of *Pardaillan et Fausta*, *Les Misérables*, and *La Légende des siècles*. I wept over Jean Valjean and Eviradnus but, the book once closed, I would erase their names from my memory and take a roll-call of my true regiment. Silvio Pellico: imprisoned for life. André Chénier: guillotined. Étienne Dolet: burned alive. Byron: dead for Greece. With icy fervour, I set about transfiguring my vocation by filling it with my old dreams; there was no stopping me: I twisted ideas, distorted the meaning of words, and cut myself off from the world for fear of bad company and comparisons. The emptiness of my soul gave place to total and permanent mobilization: I became a military dictatorship.

The uneasiness persisted in another form: I was sharpening my talent, nothing more. But what was the use of it? Men needed me: *to do what*? I was unhappy enough to question myself on my role and my destination. I asked: 'What's it really all about?' and, at once, I thought all was lost. It was about *nothing*. Not everyone who wants to can be a hero: courage and talent are not enough, there must be hydras and dragons. I could see none anywhere. Voltaire and Rousseau had slashed about hard in their time: because there were still some tyrants left. Hugo, from Guernsey, had thundered against Badinguet whom my grandfather had taught me to loathe. But I saw no merit in proclaiming my hatred, because this emperor had been dead forty years. Charles remained silent on contemporary history: this Dreyfusard never mentioned Dreyfus to me. What a pity! how eagerly I would have played the part of Zola: hissed as I left the Tribunal, I would have turned on the running-board of my carriage and broken the backs of the most excitable – no, no: I would have thought of some terrible remark which would have made them back away. And *I*, of course, would have refused to flee to England; misunderstood and neglected, what joy to become Griselda again and to tramp the streets of Paris never doubting for a moment that the Panthéon awaited me.

My grandmother used to get *Le Matin* every morning and, if I am not mistaken, *L'Excelsior*: I learnt of the existence of thieves and swindlers whom, like all decent folk, I loathed. But these tigers with human faces were not my concern: the fearless Monsieur Lépine* would suffice to checkmate them. Sometimes, the workers got angry and capital immediately took flight, but I knew nothing about it and I still do not know what my grandfather thought of it. He carried out his duties punctually as a voter, left the polling booth looking younger and slightly conceited, and, when the women teased him, 'Well, tell us who you voted for!', he would reply sharply: 'That's a man's business!' Yet, when the new President of the Republic was elected, he gave us to understand, in a moment of abandon, that he was against Pams's† candidature: 'He's a tobacco-merchant!' he exclaimed angrily. This lower middle-class intellectual wanted the top official of France to be one of his peers, a lower middle-class intellectual, Poincaré. My mother assures me today that he voted radical and that she knew all about it. This does not surprise me: he had chosen the party to which officials were drawn; and then the radicals had already outlived their day: Charles had the satisfaction of voting for a conservative party by giving his vote to a progressive one. In short, French politics, apparently, were not doing at all badly.

This really hurt me: I had armed myself to defend humanity against terrible dangers and everyone assured me that it was advancing gently towards perfection. Grandfather had brought me up to respect middle-class democracy; I would willingly have unsheathed my pen for it; but under the Presidency of Fallières‡ a peasant had the vote: what more could you ask? What does a republican do if he is lucky enough to live in a republic? He twiddles his thumbs or, rather, he teaches Greek, and describes the monuments of Aurillac in his spare time. I was back to my starting-point and I felt that I would once again

* Commissioner of Paris police at the time.
† Unsuccessful radical-socialist candidate for Presidency (1913).
‡ (Clément) Armand Fallières (1841–1931), President 1906–13.

suffocate in this world conflict which reduced the writer to idleness.

It was Charles again who got me out of difficulty. Without his knowledge, of course. Two years earlier, to open my eyes to humanism, he had expounded ideas to me of which he no longer breathed a word, for fear of encouraging my foolishness, but which were engraved on my mind. Noiselessly, they recovered their virulence and, to preserve essentials, gradually transformed the writer-knight into a writer-martyr. I have described how this failed pastor, loyal to his father's wishes, had kept the Divine and poured it into Culture. From this amalgam was born the Holy Ghost, attribute of infinite Matter, patron of literature and the arts, of classical and modern languages and of the Direct Method, a white dove which overwhelmed the Schweitzer family by its appearances, fluttered above organs and orchestras on Sundays, and, on working days, perched on my grandfather's cranium. Karl's former words, reassembled, composed a speech in my head: the world was the prey of Evil; only one salvation: to die to oneself and to the Earth, and to contemplate impossible Ideas from the depths of a shipwreck. Since no one could succeed in this without hard and dangerous training, the task had been entrusted to a body of specialists. The clergy took charge of humanity and saved it by the reversibility of merits: the wild beasts of the temporal world, great and small, had ample leisure in which to kill each other or to lead a dazed and truthless existence since writers and artists meditated in their behalf on Beauty and Goodness. To tear the entire human race from its animal state, only two conditions were required: that the relics of dead clerics – paintings, books, statues – should be preserved in supervised premises; and that at least one living cleric should remain to carry on the task and manufacture future relics.

Squalid nonsense: I swallowed it down without really understanding it, and I still believed it at twenty. Because of it, for a long time I took a work of art to be a metaphysical event whose birth interested the universe. I unearthed this fierce religion and made it my own to gild my dull vocation: I ab-

sorbed spites and acerbities which were neither mine nor my
grandfather's; the ancient bile of Flaubert, of the Goncourts,
and of Gautier poisoned me; their abstract hatred of man,
introduced into me under the disguise of love, infected me with
fresh pretensions. I became a heretic; I confused literature with
prayer and made a human sacrifice of it. My brethren, I decided,
were quite simply asking me to devote my pen to their redemp-
tion: they were suffering from an insufficiency of being which,
without the intercession of the Saints, would have doomed
them to eternal nothingness; if I opened my eyes each morning
and if, running to the window, I saw Ladies and Gentlemen still
alive passing by in the street, it was because, from dusk to dawn,
a man working in his study had struggled to write an immortal
page which earned us this reprieve of a day. He would start
again at nightfall, that evening and next day, until he died of
wear and tear; I would take over: I, too, would hold back the
human race on the brink of the abyss by my mystic offering, by
my work; the soldier was giving way smoothly to the priest: a
tragic Parsifal, I would offer myself as an expiatory victim. From
the day I discovered Chantecler,* a knot was tied in my heart:
a knot of vipers which it took thirty years to untie: torn,
bloody, and battered, this cock had found a way of protecting
an entire poultry-yard: his song was enough to rout a sparrow-
hawk, and the despicable crowd flattered him after having
mocked him; once the sparrow-hawk had vanished, the poet
returned to the fight; Beauty inspired him and multiplied his
strength; he turned on his enemy and struck him down. I wept:
I found Griselda, Corneille and Pardaillan again in one creature: Chantecler should be me. It all seemed very simple: to
write was to add another pearl to the Muses' chain, to leave to
posterity the remembrance of an exemplary life, to defend the
people against themselves and against their enemies, and to
bring down on men the blessing of heaven through a solemn
Mass. It never occurred to me that a man might write in order
to be read.

A man writes either for his neighbours or for God. I decided
to write for God with a view to saving my neighbours. I

* The cock in the play of the same name by Edmond Rostand.

wanted debtors, not readers. Contempt tainted my generosity. Already, at the time when I was protecting orphan girls, I began by getting rid of them and sending them away to hide. As a writer, my ways did not change: before I saved humanity, I would start by blindfolding it; only then would I round on the little swift, black mercenaries, on words; when my new orphan girl dared to unknot her bandage, I would be far away; saved by a single feat, she would not at first notice, blazing on a shelf in the Bibliothèque Nationale, the little brand-new volume which bore my name.

I plead extenuating circumstances. There are three. First, through a crystalline fantasy, I was questioning my right to be alive. The child, gorged with happiness and sitting bored on his perch, was recognizable in this humanity without a visa, waiting on the Artist's good pleasure; I accepted the odious myth of the Saint who saves the common people because, in the long run, the common people were me: I declared myself the licensed saviour of the crowd to achieve my own salvation discreetly and, as the Jesuits say, into the bargain.

And then I was nine years old. It did not occur to me, an only child with no companions, that my isolation could ever end. I must admit that I was a very unknown author. I had started to write again. My new novels, for want of anything better, resembled the old ones feature by feature, but no one noticed this. Not even I, who hated re-reading myself: my pen moved so rapidly that, often, my wrist ached: I would sling the filled exercise books to the floor. In the end I forgot them and they would disappear; for this reason, I never completed anything: what was the point of telling the end of a story when its beginning had got lost? Besides, if Karl had deigned to glance at these pages, he would not, in my eyes, have been a *reader* but a supreme judge and I should have been afraid that he might sentence me. Writing, my black work, referred to nothing and, all at once, became its own end: I was writing for the sake of writing. I do not regret it: if I had been read, I should have tried to please and I should have become wonderful again. In my secrecy I was real.

In the end, the idealism of the cleric was based on the realism of a child. I explained this earlier: since I had discovered the world through language, for a long time I mistook language for the world. To exist was to have a registered trade-name somewhere on the infinite Tables of the Word; writing meant engraving new beings on them or – this was my most persistent illusion – catching living things in the trap of phrases: if I put words together ingeniously, the object would become entangled in the signs, and I would hold it. In the Luxembourg Gardens, I began to be fascinated by a gleaming image of a plane tree: I did not study it; on the contrary, I trusted in space and waited; after a moment, its real foliage loomed up in the form of a simple adjective or, sometimes, a whole clause: I had enriched the universe with a mass of shimmering leaves. I never committed my discoveries to paper: they were accumulating, I thought, in my memory. In fact, I forgot them. But they gave me a glimpse of my future role: I would impose names. For several centuries, at Aurillac, some idle reams of whiteness had been crying out for fixed contours, for meaning; I would make genuine monuments of them. As a terrorist, I aimed only at their existence: I would construct it through language. As a rhetorician, I loved only words: I would raise up cathedrals of words beneath the blue gaze of the word sky. I would build for thousands of years. When I took a book, I opened and closed it in vain a score of times: I could see quite well that it did not change. Sliding across this incorruptible piece of matter, the *text*, my gaze was just a tiny event on its surface; it altered nothing and left no impression. I, on the other hand, passive and ephemeral, was a dazzled mosquito caught in a lighthouse beam; I would leave the study and put out the light: invisible in the shadows, the book continued to sparkle: for itself alone. I would give my works the violence of these corrosive fountains of light and later on, in ruined libraries, they would survive man.

I took pleasure in my obscurity; I wanted to prolong it and make a merit of it. I envied famous prisoners who had written in their dungeons on candle paper. They had kept the obligation of redeeming their contemporaries and lost that of associating with them. Naturally, progress in manners diminished my chances of drawing on my talents in seclusion, but I did not altogether despair: impressed by the modesty of my ambitions, Providence would make a point of realizing them. In the meantime, I isolated myself in anticipation.

Thwarted by my grandfather, my mother lost no opportunity of depicting my joys to come: to win me round, she put into my life all that was lacking in hers: peace, leisure, and harmony. While I was a young, still unmarried teacher, an attractive old lady would let me a comfortable room smelling of lavender and clean linen; I would bound off to the *lycée* and come back in the same way; in the evening, I would linger by my door to gossip with my landlady who would dote on me; everyone would like me, incidentally, because I had good manners and was well brought up. I heard only one word: your room. I forgot the *lycée*, a senior officer's widow, and the fusty smell; all I could see was a pool of light on my table: in the middle of a room drowned in shadow, curtains drawn, I was leaning over an exercise book bound in black cloth. My mother would go on with her story and jump ten years: an inspector-general would protect me, I should be accepted by Aurillac society, my young wife would show me the tenderest affection, I would give her good-looking and very healthy children, two sons and a daughter; she would be left some money, I would buy a site on the outskirts of the town, we would have a house built and, every Sunday, the whole family would go and inspect operations. I was not listening to a word: throughout those ten years, I would not have left my table: small, with a moustache like my father's, perched on a pile of dictionaries, my moustache would turn white, my wrist would keep moving, and one by one the exercise-books would drop to the floor. Humanity was asleep, it was night. My wife and my children were sleeping – if they were not dead. My landlady was asleep. Sleep had banished me from all their minds. What loneliness: two thousand million men stretched out and myself, up above them, sole look-out.

The Holy Ghost would look at me. He had just decided to ascend to Heaven again and abandon men; I should barely have time to offer myself. I would show him the wounds of my soul and the tears soaking my sheet of paper; he would read over my shoulder and his anger would abate. Was he appeased by the depth of my sufferings or by the magnificence of the work? I said to myself: by the work; but, on the sly, I thought: by my sufferings. Of course the Holy Ghost appreciated only *truly* artistic writing, but I had read Musset and I knew that '*les plus désespérés sont les chants les plus beaux*'* and I had decided to catch Beauty in the trap of despair. I had always found the word genius suspect: I even came to loathe it altogether. Where would be the anguish, the ordeal, the temptation resisted, even the merit, if I had gifts? I found it hard to have a body and every day the same head, and I was not going to let myself be confined in any sort of equipment. I accepted my appointment on condition that it depended on nothing, that it shone, gratuitously, in absolute space. I held secret meetings with the Holy Ghost: 'You will write,' he told me. And I would wring my hands: 'What is there about me, Lord, that you should choose me?' 'Nothing special.' 'Then, why me?' 'No reason.' 'Have I at least some facility with the pen?' 'None. Do you think great works grow from facile pens?' 'Lord, since I am of so little account, how could I produce a book?' 'Through diligence.' 'So anyone can write?' 'Anyone, but you are the one I have chosen.' This was a most convenient bit of cheating: it enabled me to proclaim my insignificance and simultaneously to esteem in myself the author of future masterpieces. I was chosen, singled out but without talent: everything would derive from my long patience and from my misfortunes; I denied myself all singularity: my traits of character sat awkwardly. I was loyal only to the sovereign engagement which led me to glory through torments. I still had to find these torments; this was the one and only problem but it seemed insoluble because I had been robbed of all hope of living in poverty: famous or obscure, I would draw my salary from the Teaching estimates, and I would never be hungry. I promised myself fearful love-agonies, but without enthusiasm: I hated bashful lovers. Cyrano, that pseudo-Pardaillan who said foolish things before women, shocked me: the real one dragged all

* 'The most despairing songs are the most beautiful.'

hearts behind him without so much as a thought for them; it is true to say that the death of Violetta, his mistress, had cut him to the heart for ever. A widowerhood and an incurable wound – because, yes, because of a woman, but not through fault of hers: that would enable me to repel the advances of all the rest. To be gone into. But, anyhow, even allowing that my young Aurillac bride might disappear in an accident, this misfortune would not be sufficient to make me elect: it was at the same time fortuitous and too common. My fury carried the day; mocked and defeated, certain authors had cowered in shame and darkness until their last breath and glory had crowned only their corpses: this was how I should be. I would write conscientiously about Aurillac and its statues. Incapable of hatred, I would attempt only to reconcile and to serve. Yet, as soon as it appeared, my first book would create a scandal and I would become a public enemy: I would be insulted by the newspapers of Auvergne; shopkeepers would refuse to serve me, and fanatics would throw stones at my windows; to avoid being lynched, I should have to run away. Dumbfounded at first, I would spend months in a daze, repeating endlessly: 'It's only a misunderstanding, you know! Because everyone's good!' And it would in fact be only a misunderstanding, but the Holy Ghost would not allow it to be cleared up. I would recover; one day, I would sit at my table and write a new book: at sea or in the mountains. It would not find a publisher. Pursued, disguised, perhaps outlawed, I would write others, many others. I would translate Horace into verse and I would expound modest and extremely reasonable ideas about teaching. In vain: my exercise-books would pile up in a trunk, unpublished.

The story had two endings; I chose one or other according to my mood. On my disgruntled days, I would see myself dying on an iron bedstead, hated by all, in despair, at the very hour when Glory was raising its trumpet to its mouth. At other times, I granted myself a little happiness. At the age of fifty, to try out a new pen, I would write my name on a manuscript which, shortly afterwards, would get lost. Someone would find it, in an attic, in a stream, or in the cupboard of a house I had just left, and he would read it; knocked sideways, he would take it along to Arthème Fayard, Michel Zévaco's famous publisher. It would be a triumph: ten thousand copies snapped up in two days. What remorse in people's hearts! A hundred reporters would start out in search of me but would not find me. A recluse, I would long remain unaware of this veering of opinion. Eventually, one day, I would go into a café to shelter from the rain, I would espy a magazine lying there, and what should I see? 'Jean-Paul Sartre, the hidden writer, the bard of Aurillac, the poet of the sea.' On the third page, across six columns, in capitals. I would exult. No: I would be exquisitely sad. In any case, I would go back home and, with the help of my landlady, lock and rope the trunk full of exercise-books and send it to Fayard without my address. At this point in my story, I would break off to soar away on some delicious flight of fancy. If I sent the parcel from the town where I was living, the journalists would be quick to discover my retreat. So I would take the trunk to Paris and leave it with the porter at the publishing-house; before catching the train, I would return to my childhood haunts, the rue le Goff, the rue Soufflot and the Luxembourg Gardens. The 'Balzar' would attract me; I would remember that my grandfather – since dead – had taken me there sometimes, in 1913: we would sit side by side on the seat, everyone would look at us with an air of complicity, he would order a *bock* and a small glass of beer for me and I would feel loved. So, a nostalgic fifty-year old, I would push open the door of the *brasserie* and I would order myself a glass. At the next table, some young, attractive women, chatting brightly, would mention my name. 'Ah!' one of them would say, 'he may be old, he may be ugly, but what does it matter: I'd give thirty years of my life to be his wife!' I would give her a proud but sad smile, she would reply with a smile of astonishment, and I would get up and disappear.

I spent a lot of time embroidering on this incident and a hundred others which I will spare the reader. My actual childhood, my situation, the fantasies of my sixth year, and the sulks of my misunderstood knights can be recognized, projected into the future. I was still sulking, at nine, and derived intense pleasure from it: by sulking, I preserved, a martyr to the last, a misunderstanding of which even the Holy Ghost himself seemed weary. Why did I not tell my name to that delightful woman admirer? Ah! I told myself, she has come too late. But since she has accepted me anyhow? Well, then, it is because I am too poor. Too poor? How about your royalties? This objection did not stop me: I had written to Fayard telling him to distribute the money due to me among the poor. Yet I had to round things off: ah, well! I would pass away in my little room, abandoned by everyone but serene: mission accomplished.

One thing strikes me in this oft-repeated story: the day I saw my name in the paper, a spring broke and I was finished; I enjoyed my fame sadly but I stopped writing. The two endings are but one: whether I died to be born to glory or glory came first and killed me, the urge to write contained a refusal to live. About that time, a story, read I know not where, disturbed me: it is set in the last century; a writer is taking a stroll at a Siberian halt while he waits for a train. Not a hovel as far as the horizon; not a living soul. The writer carries his large, gloomy head with difficulty. He is short-sighted, unmarried, unmannerly and always in a temper; he is bored and is worrying about his prostate, about his debts. A young countess appears, in a closed carriage, on the road running alongside the track: she jumps out of the carriage, runs to the traveller whom she has never seen but pretends to recognize from a daguerreotype she has been shown. She bows, takes his right hand and kisses it. The story ended there, and I have no idea what it was meant to convey. At the age of nine, I was amazed that this surly author should find women-readers in the steppes and that such an attractive person should come and remind him of the glory which he had forgotten: it was like being born. Deeper down, it was like dying: I felt it, I wanted it so; a commoner today could not receive such evidence of admiration from an aristocrat. The countess seemed to be saying: 'I have been able to come to you and touch you because I have no need to maintain my superiority of rank any longer. I am not even worried about what you think of my gesture; I no longer see you as a man but as the symbol of your work.' Killed by a kiss on the hand: a thousand versts from St Petersburg, fifty-five years after his birth, a traveller caught fire and his glory consumed him, leaving only, in letters of flame, the catalogue of his works. I saw the countess get back into her carriage and disappear; the steppe reverted to its loneliness; at dusk, the train would shoot past the halt to make up for lost time. I would feel, in the pit of my stomach, a tremor of fear, and would remember *Du Vent dans les arbres* as I thought: 'The Countess was death.' She would come: one day, on a deserted road, she would kiss my fingers.

I was intoxicated by death because I did not like life: this explains the terror with which it inspired me. Identifying it with glory, I made it my goal. I wanted to die; sometimes horror chilled my impatience: never for long; my sacred joy would be reborn, and I would wait for the lightning flash when I should go up in flames. Our deepest intentions are an inextricable web of plans and evasions; I can see that my mad undertaking to write in order to be forgiven for being alive had, in spite of lies and cowardice, some validity: the proof is that I am still writing, fifty years later. But if I probe into the origins, I can see in them a flight forward and a suicide à la Gribouille*; yes, what I was seeking, more than the epic, more than martyrdom, was death. I had long been afraid of ending up as I had begun, somewhere or other, somehow or other, and that this vague death would be merely the reflection of my vague birth. My vocation changed everything: sword-play vanished, writing remained, and I discovered that the Giver, in Belles-Lettres, can change himself into his own Gift; that is to say, into a pure object. Chance had made me a man, generosity would make me a book. I could let my chatter and my consciousness flow into characters of bronze, replace the sounds of my life by imperishable inscriptions, my flesh by a style, and the languid spirals of Time by eternity. I could appear to the Holy Spirit as a precipitate of language, become an obsession for the human race and at last be *other*, other than myself, other than others, other than everything. I would start by giving myself an everlasting body

* A character of folklore who jumped into the river to avoid getting wet in the rain.

and then yield myself up to the perfectors. I would not write for the pleasure of writing but to carve this glorious body in words. Viewed from the heights of my tomb, I saw my birth as a necessary evil, a purely temporary incarnation that was making ready for my transfiguration: to be reborn you had to write and to write you needed a brain, eyes, and arms. Your work done, these organs would be reabsorbed into themselves: round about 1955, a larva would burst and twenty-five folio butterflies would escape, feverishly beating their pages, and settle on a shelf in the Bibliothèque Nationale. These butterflies would be none other than myself. Me: twenty-five volumes, eighteen thousand pages of text and three hundred illustrations, including a portrait of the author. My bones are leather and cardboard, my parchment flesh smells of glue and mildew, and I strut at my ease across a hundredweight or so of paper. I am reborn, I have at last become a complete man, thinking, speaking, singing, thundering, and asserting himself with the peremptory inertia of matter. I am taken up, opened out, spread on the table, smoothed with the flat of the hand and sometimes made to crack. I let it happen and then suddenly I flash, dazzle, impose myself from a distance; my powers traverse space and time, strike down the wicked and protect the good. No one can forget me or pass me over in silence: I am a large, manageable, and terrible fetish. My consciousness is in fragments: all the better. Other consciousnesses have taken charge of me. They read *me* and I leap to their eyes; they talk about *me* and I am on everyone's lips, a universal and singular language; I have made myself a prospective interest for millions of glances. For anyone who knows how to like me, I am his most intimate disquiet: but if he wants to touch me, I draw aside and vanish: I exist nowhere but I *am*, at last! I am everywhere: a parasite on humanity, by my good deeds I prey on it and force it endlessly to revive my absence.

This conjuring-trick succeeded: I buried death in the shroud of glory. I thought only of the glory, never of death, without reflecting that the two were one. Now, as I write these lines, I know that I have had my time to within a few years. Now, I can picture to myself clearly, but not too cheerfully, the approach of age and my future decline, the decline and death of those I love; but my own death, never. I sometimes hint to those around me – some of whom are fifteen, twenty, even thirty years younger than I am – how sorry I shall be to outlive them: they make fun of me and I laugh with them, but nothing happens and nothing will happen: when I was nine, an operation removed my capacity for feeling that sense of the pathetic thought proper to our condition. Ten years later, at the École Normale, this sense woke, with a start, some of my best friends in either terror or rage: I continued to snore soundly. After a serious illness, one of them assured us that he had known the horrors of the death-agony, up to and including the last breath. Nizan was the most obsessed: sometimes, in the centre of the city, he would see himself as a corpse; he would get up, his eyes swarming with worms, grope for his round-brimmed Borsalino, and disappear; next day we would find him drunk, among strangers. Sometimes, these condemned men, gathered in a study, would tell each other about their sleepless nights and their anticipated experiences of nothingness: they understood each other without explanation. I used to listen to them, I liked them enough to want passionately to be one of them, but it was no good, I could not catch on, and all I retained were some commonplaces about being buried: you live, you die, you do not know who is living or who is dying; an hour before death, you are still alive. I did not question that their talk had some meaning which escaped me; I was jealous and I fell silent, in exile. In the end, they would turn to me, already irritated. 'All this leaves you cold?' I would spread my arms in a gesture of helplessness and humility. They would laugh with rage, blinded by the shattering evidence which they had failed to convey to me. 'Hasn't it ever occurred to you, as you dropped off, that there were people who would die during their sleep? Haven't you ever thought, as you brushed your teeth: this is it, this time, this is my last day? Haven't you ever felt that you had to move fast, really fast, and that you were short of time? Do you think you're immortal?' I would reply, half-defiantly and half from habit: 'That's it: I think I'm immortal.' Nothing was less true; I had forearmed myself against accidental death, that was all; the Holy Ghost had commissioned a long-term work from me, so he had to give me time to complete it. It was my death, a glorious death, which preserved me from jumping the metals, strokes and peritonitis; death and I had made a date; if I arrived too early for the appointment, I should not find it there; my friends might well reproach me for never thinking about it: they did not know that I never for a moment stopped living it.

Today, I see that they were right: they had accepted everything in our lot, even anxiety; I had chosen to be reassured; and it was quite true that, deep down, I believed myself to be immortal: I had killed myself in advance because only the dead can enjoy immortality. Nizan and Maheu knew that they would be the victims of savage aggression, that they would be torn alive and full-blooded from the world. But I was lying to myself: to remove the barbarity from death, I had made it my goal, and my life the one and only known means of dying. I was moving quietly towards my end, hoping and wishing only for what was necessary to fill my books, confident that the last flutter of my heart would be recorded on the last page of the last volume of my works and that death would take away only a dead man. At twenty, Nizan looked on women and cars and all this world's possessions with the haste of a desperate man: he had to see everything, take everything straight away. I looked, too, but with more zeal than covetousness: I was not on earth to enjoy things but to draw up a balance-sheet. It was a little too convenient: through cowardice, and the timidity of a too well-behaved child, I had recoiled before the dangers of an existence that was open, free, and without guarantees from providence, and I had convinced myself that everything was decreed in advance or, better still, had already happened.

Naturally this fraudulent device spared me the temptations of self-love. Threatened with extinction, each of my friends barricaded himself in the present, discovered the irreplaceable quality of his mortal life and deemed himself touching, precious and unique; each of them liked himself; I, the dead man, did not like myself: I found myself very ordinary, more boring than the great Corneille, and my singularity as a subject seemed in my eyes to have no other point than to prepare for the moment which would change me into an object. Was I more modest in this? No, more cunning: I was compelling my descendants to love me in my place, and, for men and women still unborn, I would one day have charm, a special something, and I would make them happy. I was even more artful and sly: I came back in secret to this life, which I found tedious and which I had been able to fashion only into the instrument of my death, in order to save it; I looked at it through future eyes and it seemed to me a moving and wonderful story which I had lived on behalf of everyone, which no one, thanks to me, would ever have to relive and which it was enough to describe. I set about this with genuine fervour: I chose for a future the past of a famous dead man, and I tried to live backwards. Between the ages of nine and ten, I became entirely posthumous.

It was not altogether my fault: my grandfather had brought me up in a retrospective illusion. But he was not guilty, either, and I do not bear him the slightest resentment: this mirage was born spontaneously from culture. When its witnesses have disappeared, the death of a great man is no longer a sudden disaster; time makes it a trait of character. A man long since dead is dead by his very nature; he is no more and no less dead at his baptism than at extreme unction; his life is ours; we enter it at one end, at the other, or in the middle, and we go up or down its course at will: it is because the chronological order has gone to pieces; impossible to reassemble it: this person runs no further risk and no longer even waits for the tickling in his nostril to end in a sneeze. His existence looks like an unfolding, but, as soon as you try to breathe a little life into it, it reverts to simultaneity. It is no good putting yourself in the dead man's shoes, pretending to share his passions, his blunders, and his prejudices, reawakening vanished moments of strength, impatience, or apprehension; you cannot help assessing his behaviour in the light of results which he could not foresee and of information which he did not possess, or attributing a particular solemnity to events whose effects marked him later, but which he lived through casually. That is the mirage: the future more real than the present. It is not surprising: in a completed life, the end is taken as the truth of the beginning. The dead man stands half-way between being and worth, between the crude fact and its reconstruction: his history becomes a kind of circular essence which is summed up in each of his moments. In the drawing-rooms of Arras, a cold and affected young lawyer is carrying his head under his arm because he is the late Robespierre; the head is dripping blood, though it does not stain the carpet; not one of the guests notices it yet we see nothing else; some five years go by before it rolled into the basket, and yet there it is, chopped off, making gallant speeches, in spite of its sagging jaw. Recognized, this optical illusion is not hampering: we have the means to correct it; but the clerics of the time concealed it and used it to nourish their idealism. When a great thought wishes to be born, they would imply, it commandeers, in the womb of some woman, the great man who is to bear it; it chooses his condition, his milieu, it calculates the precise level of intelligence and incomprehension of those around him, arranges his education, submits him to the required tests, and produces, with successive touches, an unstable character, governing its lack of balance until the object of so much care bursts in giving birth to it. This was nowhere stated but everything would suggest that the chain of causes conceals an inverse and secret order.

I used this mirage enthusiastically to be sure of guaranteeing my fate. I took my time, stood it on its head and everything became clear. It began with a small midnight-blue book with tawdry, rather darkened gold ornamentation, whose thick leaves smelt like a corpse and which was entitled: *L'Enfance des hommes illustres* (the childhood of famous men). A book-plate testified that my uncle Georges had won it in 1885, as second prize in arithmetic. I had discovered it, at the time of my eccentric travels, turned over the leaves, and then flung it away in annoyance: these young elect bore no resemblance to infant prodigies; they were like me only in the feebleness of their virtues, and I wondered why they were talked about. In the end the book disappeared: I had decided to punish it by hiding it. A year later, I turned all the shelves upside down to find it again: I had changed, and the infant prodigy had become a great man victimized by childhood. What a surprise: the book had changed, too. They were the same words, but they were telling me about myself. I had a presentiment that this work was going to ruin me; I hated it and I was afraid of it. Each day, before opening it, I would go and sit by the window: in case of danger, I would let the true light of day enter into my eyes. Today, people make me laugh when they deplore the influence of Fantômas or of André Gide: can they suppose that children do not choose their own poisons? I gulped mine down with the grim austerity of a drug-addict. Yet it seemed harmless enough. Young readers were encouraged: good behaviour and filial piety were the basis of everything – led even to becoming Rembrandt or Mozart; short stories retraced the very normal occupations of boys no less normal, but sensitive and pious, who were called Johann Sebastian, Jean-Jacques or Jean-Baptiste, and who brought happiness to their near relations as I did to mine. But here was the poison: without ever mentioning the name Rousseau, Bach, or Molière, the author deployed his skill in planting allusions everywhere to their future greatness, recalling casually, by some detail, their most famous works or actions, and arranging his narrative so that you could not grasp the most trivial incident without relating it to subsequent events; into the tumult of daily life, he brought a vast, fabulous silence which transfigured everything: the future. A certain Sanzio was dying to see the pope; he worked it so well that he was led into the public square one day as the Holy Father was passing; the boy turned pale, stared wide-eyed, and eventually someone said to him: 'You seem happy, Raffaello. I hope you had a good look at the Holy Father?' But he answered, his face drawn: 'What Holy Father? All I saw was colours!' Another day, little Miguel, who wanted to take up soldiering, was sitting under a tree and enjoying a romance of chivalry when, suddenly, a clatter of metal startled him: it was an old madman, a ruined country gentleman of the vicinity, cara-colling along on a jade and pointing his rusty lance at a wind-mill. At dinner, Miguel related the incident with such sweet and amusing facial expressions that he had everyone in stitches;

but, later on, alone in his room, he flung his romance to the floor, trampled on it, and sobbed for a long time.

These children lived in error: they thought they were acting and speaking fortuitously whereas the true goal of their most trivial remarks was to proclaim their Destiny. The author and I exchanged moving smiles above their heads; I read the lives of these false mediocrities as God had envisaged them: beginning at the end. At first, I triumphed: they were my brothers and their glory would be mine. And then everything rocked: I found myself on the other side of the page, *in the book*: Jean-Paul's childhood was like those of Jean-Jacques and Johann Sebastian, and nothing happened to him that was not for the most part a foreshadowing. Only this time the author was winking at my great-nephews. I was being looked at, from death to birth, by these children to come whom I could not imagine and to whom I kept sending messages which I could not myself decipher. I shuddered, chilled by my death, the true meaning of all my actions and, dispossessed of myself, I tried to recross the page in the opposite direction and rejoin the readers' side; I looked up and asked help of the light: yet *that too* was a message; that sudden anxiety, that doubt, that movement of the eyes and neck, how would they be interpreted in 2013, when the two keys which would open me, my work and my death, were available? There was no way out of the book: I had finished reading it long since, but I remained one of its characters. I began to examine myself: an hour earlier I had been prattling with my mother: what had I said? I recalled a few of my words and repeated them aloud, but that did not get me any further. The sentences, inscrutable, glided along, my voice rang in my ears like a stranger's, a thieving angel was pirating my thoughts, from my very head, and this angel was simply a fair-haired thirtieth-century boy, sitting by a window, watching me through a book. With a mixture of love and horror, I felt his gaze pin me to my millenium. I faked myself for him: I invented words with double meanings and let them out in public. Anne-Marie found me scribbling away at my desk and said: 'How dark it's getting! My little darling will ruin his eyes.' This was an opportunity to reply in all innocence: 'I can write even in the dark.' She laughed and called me a little fool, put on the light, the trick had worked, and neither of us knew that I had just informed the year three thousand of my future infirmity. In fact, towards the end of my life, blinder even than Beethoven was deaf, I would put my final work together gropingly: the manuscript would be found among my papers and people would say, disappointed: 'But it's illegible!' There would even be talk of flinging it into the dustbin. In the end, it would be claimed by the Aurillac town library out of sheer piety and would remain there a hundred years, forgotten. And then, one day, for love of me, some young scholars would try to decipher it: their whole lives would not be too long for the reconstruction of what, naturally, would be my masterpiece. My mother had left the room and I was alone; I said over to myself, slowly, and certainly without thinking, 'In the dark!' There would be a sharp clap: my great-great-nephew up there would be closing his book: he would be thinking of his great-great-uncle's childhood, and tears would be rolling down his cheeks: 'But it's true,' he would say with a sigh, 'he did write in the dark!'

I paraded before children yet unborn who resembled me feature for feature and I wrung tears from myself by imagining those I would make them shed. I saw my death through their eyes; it had taken place, and it was my true self: I am my own obituary notice.

After reading the above lines, a friend looked at me anxiously: 'You were,' he said, 'even more affected than I thought.' Affected? I am not so sure. My madness was patently calculated. In my view, the major question would be one of sincerity. At the age of nine, I remained well within it; afterwards I went far beyond it.

At first, I was sound as a bell: a little humbug who knew how to stop in time. But I stuck at it: I remained a good scholar even in bluff; today, I see my conjuring-tricks as spiritual exercises and my insincerity as caricature of a total sincerity which was constantly brushing against me and eluding me. I had not *chosen* my vocation: others had imposed it on me. In fact, nothing had happened: chance words, tossed off by an old lady, and Charles's machiavellism. But it was enough that I was convinced. The grown-ups, established in my soul, pointed a finger at my star; I did not see it but I saw their fingers; I believed in these people who pretended to believe in me. They had taught me the existence of the famous dead – one of them yet to come – Napoleon, Themistocles, Philip Augustus, Jean-Paul Sartre. ... I had no doubts: it would have been like doubting them. I would simply have liked to meet the last-named face to face. I gaped, I tied myself in knots to provoke the intuition which would have satisfied me; I was a frigid woman whose convulsions first invite and then try to replace an orgasm. Should it be said she is dissembling or just trying rather too hard? In any event, I obtained nothing. I was always in front of or behind the impossible vision which would have revealed me to myself and I found, after my exertions, that I was uncertain and had gained nothing except a good deal of nervous irritation. Nothing could affirm or give the lie to my mandate, which was based on the principle of authority and on the undeniable kindness of the grown-ups: out of reach, sealed up, it remained within me, but belonged to me so little that I never had been able, even for a moment, to doubt it, nor was I capable of dissolving it and assimilating it.

Faith, even when profound, is never complete. It has to be endlessly sustained or, at least, preserved from destruction. I was dedicated and famous, *I had* my tomb in the Père-Lachaise cemetery – perhaps even in the Panthéon, my avenue in Paris, my squares and *places* in the provinces and abroad: yet, in the very heart of my optimism, I retained an invisible and nameless suspicion of my lack of substance. In Sainte-Anne's Asylum, a sick man shouted from his bed: 'I'm a prince! Put the Grand Duke under arrest.' Someone went up to him and whispered: 'Wipe your nose!' and he wiped it; he was asked: 'What's your trade?' and he replied softly: 'A shoemaker,' and started shouting again. We are all like that man, I imagine; certainly I was like him when I entered my ninth year: I was both prince and shoemaker.

Two years later, you would have thought me cured: the prince had vanished, the shoemaker believed in nothing; and I had even stopped writing; the exercise-books for novels, flung in the dustbin, lost or burnt, had given place to others full of logical analysis, dictations, and arithmetic. If someone had been able to enter into my head, exposed to the four winds, he would have found a few busts, a faulty multiplication table and the rule of three, thirty-two departments with chief towns but no sub-prefectures, a rose called rosarosarosamrosaerosaerosa, some historic and literary monuments, a few polite maxims engraved on steles, and, sometimes – a scarf of mist trailing above this sad garden – a sadistic day-dream. No orphaned girl. No sign of any knights in armour. The words of hero, martyr and saint were not inscribed anywhere nor echoed by any voice. Each school term, the ex-Pardaillan received satisfactory health bulletins: a child of average intelligence and of very good conduct, not gifted in the exact sciences, imaginative within reason, and sensitive; perfectly normal except for a certain affectedness already on the wane. Yet I had become mad. Two events, one public and one private, had blown away the little sense I had left.

The first was a genuine surprise: in July 1914, there were still a few wicked people about; but on 2 August, virtue suddenly seized power and reigned: all Frenchmen became good. My grandfather's enemies flung themselves into his arms, publishers joined up and the common people made prophecies: our friends garnered noble yet simple remarks from their *concierges*, postmen and plumbers, passed them on to us and everyone cried out, except my grandmother, who was distinctly dubious. I was enraptured. France was providing me with a comedy and I was acting it for France. Yet the war soon bored me: it altered my life so little that I would probably have forgotten it; but I came to detest it when I noticed that it was spoiling my reading. My favourite publications disappeared from the paper-stalls; Arnould Galopin, Jo Valle, and Jean de la Hire deserted their usual heroes, those adolescents, my brothers, who went round the world by biplane and seaplane and who fought, two or three against a hundred; the pre-war colonial novels gave place to warlike novels, full of cabin-boys, young Alsatians and orphans, and regimental mascots. I loathed these newcomers. I saw the young adventurers of the jungle as infant prodigies because they massacred natives who are, after all, adults: in them I recognized myself, also an infant prodigy. But everything happened around those children of the barracks. Individual heroism wavered: it was maintained against the savages by superiority of arms; but what could you do against German field-guns? You needed other field-guns, gunners and an army. In the company of the brave troopers who patted him on the head and protected him, the infant prodigy fell back into childhood; I fell back with him. From time to time, the author, out of pity, would entrust me with a message, the Germans would capture me, I would make a few proud rejoinders and then escape, regain our lines and complete my mission. I was congratulated, of course, but without genuine enthusiasm, and I did not find in the general's fatherly eyes the dazzled glances of widows and orphans. I had lost the initiative: battles were being won and the war would be won without me; the grown-ups were recovering the monopoly of heroism; I might happen to pick up a dead man's rifle and fire a few shots, but Arnould Galopin or Jean de la Hire would never allow me to charge with a bayonet. An apprentice hero, I waited impatiently to be old enough to enlist. Well, not really: it was the child of the barracks, the orphan from Alsace who was waiting. I drew away from them and closed the magazine. Writing would be a long, unrewarding task, I knew; I would have the patience of Job. But reading was a pleasure: I wanted all the glories straight off. What future was offered me? To be a soldier? Was that all? On his own, the private counted little more than a child. He went into the attack with the rest, and it was the regiment that won the battle. I was not interested in taking part in community victories. When Arnould Galopin wanted to single out a private, he could find nothing better than to send him to the aid of a wounded captain. This obscure devotion annoyed me: the slave was rescuing his master. Anyway, it was only a second-rate exploit: in time of war, courage is the most widely spread attribute; with a little luck, any other private would have done as much. I was furious. What I preferred in pre-war heroism was that it was lonely and disinterested: I was turning my back on pale, everyday virtues and was creating a man for myself alone, out of generosity; *Le Tour du monde en hydravion*, *Les Aventures d'un gamin de Paris*, and *Les Trois boy scouts*, all these sacred texts were guiding me along the path of death and resurrection. And now, suddenly, their authors had betrayed me: they had set heroism within anyone's grasp: courage and self-sacrifice were becoming humdrum virtues; worse still, they were being reduced to the level of the most elementary duties. The change of décor was in the image of this transformation: the collective mists of the Argonne had replaced the large, unique sun and individualistic light of the Equator.

After a gap of a few months, I decided to take up my pen again to write a novel after my own heart and teach these Gentlemen a lesson. It was in October 1914 and we had not left Arcachon. My mother bought me some exercise-books, all similar; on their mauve covers was Joan of Arc in a helmet, a sign of the times. Under the Maid's protection, I began the story of Private Perrin: he captured the Kaiser, led him bound into our lines and then, before the assembled regiment, challenged him to single combat, struck him down and forced him, a knife at his throat, to sign an ignominious peace, and hand back Alsace-Lorraine to us. After a week the tale bored me stiff. I had borrowed the idea of the duel from cloak-and-dagger romances: Stoerte-Becker, of good family but outlawed, entered a wine-shop full of rogues; insulted by a Hercules, the leader of the gang, he killed him with his fists, took his place and went out again, king of the hooligans, just in time to put his troops aboard a pirate ship. Strict, immutable laws governed the ceremony: the champion of Evil had to appear invincible whereas the champion of Good had to be hissed as he fought and his unexpected victory had to chill the jeering onlookers with terror. But in my inexperience, I had infringed all the rules and done the opposite of what I intended: however tough he might be, the Kaiser was not a heavyweight; it was obvious in advance that Perrin, a superb athlete, would make short work of him. And then the audience was hostile to the Kaiser; our *poilus* shouted their hatred of him: by means of a reversal which left me aghast, William 11, criminal but alone, covered with spit and insults, usurped, before my very eyes, the regal isolation of my heroes.

Worse was to follow. Until then, nothing had either confirmed or challenged what Louise called my 'lucubrations': Africa was vast, distant, under-populated, and little was known about it: no one was in a position to prove that my explorers were not there, that they were not skirmishing with the pygmies at the very moment I was recounting their struggle. I did not go so far as to imagine that I was their chronicler, but I had been told so much about the truth of romantic works that I thought I was telling the truth in my fictions, in a way that still escaped me but which would spring to the eyes of my future readers. Now, in this ill-omened month of October, I was present but helpless at a telescoping of fiction and reality: the Kaiser born of my pen, defeated, ordered the cease-fire; so, for the sake of logic, the autumn *had* to see the return of peace; but then newspapers and adults kept on saying day and night that the war was settling down and that it was going to last. I felt perplexed: I was an impostor and I was relating nonsense that no one would want to believe; in short, I discovered the imagination. For the first time in my life I re-read myself. Scarlet in the face. Was this really me, *me* taking pleasure in these childish fantasies? I very nearly renounced literature. In the end, I took my exercise-book to the beach and buried it in the sand. My uneasiness faded; I regained confidence: I was unquestionably dedicated; it was merely that Belles-Lettres had their secret and one day would reveal it to me. In the meantime, my age compelled me to extreme caution. I stopped writing.

We returned to Paris. I gave up Arnould Galopin and Jean de la Hire for good: I could not forgive these opportunists for being right at my expense. I sulked over the war, epic of mediocrity; embittered, I walked out on the age and took refuge in the past. A few months earlier, at the end of 1913, I had discovered *Nick Carter*, *Buffalo Bill*, *Texas Jack*, and *Sitting Bull*. When hostilities opened, these publications ceased: my grandfather asserted that the publisher was German. Luckily, most of the parts which had appeared were to be found on the second-hand stalls on the *quais*. I dragged my mother down to the banks of the Seine, and we set out to search the stalls one by one from the Gare d'Orsay to the Gare d'Austerlitz: we sometimes brought back fifteen instalments at a time; I soon had five hundred. I would sort them into equal heaps and never tired of counting them and saying their mysterious titles loud: *Un Crime en ballon, Le Pacte avec le diable, Les Esclaves du Baron Moutoushimi, La Résurrection de Dazaar.* I liked them for being yellow, stained, and dog's-eared, with a peculiar smell of dead leaves: *they were* dead leaves, decayed things, because the war had put a stop to them all; I knew that the final adventure of the man with long hair would remain for ever closed to me, and that I would never know about the last investigation of the king of the detectives: these lonely heroes were like myself, victims of the world conflict, and I liked them all the more for it. All I had to do to go wild with delight was to look at the coloured illustrations on the covers. Buffalo Bill, on horseback, would be galloping through the prairie, sometimes pursuing, sometimes pursued by the Indians. I preferred the illustrations of Nick Carter. They might be thought monotonous: in nearly all of them the great detective is felling someone or is himself being bludgeoned. But these brawls were taking place in the streets of Manhattan, waste land, enclosed by brown wooden fences or frail cubic buildings the colour of dried blood: that fascinated me. I imagined a puritan and bloody city devoured by space and barely concealing the savannah which lay beneath it: crime and virtue were both outside the law there; the assassin and the representative of justice, each of them free and sovereign, had it out in the evenings, with knives. In that city, as in Africa, under the same blazing sun, heroism again became an endless improvisation: hence my passion for New York.

I forgot simultaneously the war and my mandate. When I was asked: 'What will you do when you grow up?' I would answer pleasantly and modestly that I would write, but I had given up my dreams of glory and my spiritual exercises. Thanks to this, perhaps, the war years were the happiest of my childhood. My mother and I were the same age and we never left each other's side. She used to call me her attendant knight and her little man; I told her everything. More than everything: inside me once again, my writing turned to babble and issued from my mouth: I described what I saw – what Anne-Marie saw as clearly as I did: the houses, the trees, the people. I gave myself feelings for the pleasure of sharing them with her, and I became a transformer of energy: the world made use of me as a mouthpiece. It began with an anonymous flow of chatter in my head: someone would be saying: 'I'm walking, I'm sitting down, I'm drinking a glass of water, I'm eating a burnt almond.' I would repeat out loud this everlasting commentary: 'I'm walking, *maman*, I'm drinking a glass of water, I'm sitting down.' I thought I had two voices; one – which hardly belonged to me and was not dependent on my will – was dictating to the other what to say. I decided that I was dual. These trivial anxieties persisted until the summer: they wore me out, I got annoyed with them and in the end took fright. 'There's talking in my head,' I told my mother who, luckily, was not worried.

This did not spoil my happiness or our intimacy. We had our myths, our habits of speech, and our ritual jokes. For almost a year, I ended my sentences, at least one in every ten, with these words, spoken with ironic resignation: 'But it doesn't matter.' I would say: 'There's a big white dog. He's not white, he's grey, but it doesn't matter.' We acquired the habit of recounting to each other in epic form the details of our life as they occurred; we referred to ourselves in the third person plural. We would be waiting for the bus and it would pass us without stopping; one of us would then exclaim: 'They stamped the earth and cursed the heavens,' and we would start to laugh. In public, we had our little conspiracies: a wink was enough. In a store or a tea-shop, the assistant would strike us as comic and my mother would say to me as we went out: 'I didn't look at you, I was afraid I'd burst out laughing in her face,' and I would feel proud of my power: there were not so many children who could make their mothers burst out laughing with a single glance. We were shy and nervous together: one day, on the *quais*, I discovered a dozen numbers of *Buffalo Bill* which I had not yet got; she was about to pay for them, when a man came

136

up, pale and fat, with coal-black eyes, a waxed moustache, a boater and that edible look favoured by handsome young men of the time. He stared at my mother but it was to me he spoke: 'You're spoilt, boy, you're spoilt!' he kept saying quickly. At first, I merely took offence: I was not used to being spoken to familiarly so soon; but I caught his mad look, and Anne-Marie and I quickly became a single terrified young girl who sprang backwards. The man was disconcerted and went away: I have forgotten thousands of faces, but I still remember that pasty complexion; I knew nothing of the flesh and I had no idea what the man wanted but the evidence of desire was so strong that I seemed to understand and, in some way or other, everything was revealed to me. I sensed his desire through Anne-Marie; through her, I learned to scent the male, to fear and loathe him. This incident bound us more closely together: I used to trot along looking tough, my hand in my mother's, confident that I could protect her. Is it the memory of those years? Even today, I cannot see an over-solemn child talking gravely and affectionately to its child mother without pleasure; I like these gentle yet shy friendships which spring up far away from men and against them. I stare at these childlike couples for a long time, and then I remember that I am a man and look away.

The second event took place in October 1915: I was ten years and three months old, and they could not think of keeping me sequestrated any longer. Charles Schweitzer muzzled his grudges and entered me at the junior Lycée Henri IV as a day-boy.

I came bottom in my first essay. A young feudal type, I considered teaching a personal bond: Mademoiselle Marie-Louise had given me her knowledge out of love, and I had received it out of kindness, out of love for her. I was disconcerted by these *ex cathedra* lessons intended for everyone and by the democratic coldness of the law. Subjected to endless comparisons, my fancied superiorities faded; there was always someone who answered more quickly or better than I did. I was too well loved to doubt myself: I admired my companions wholeheartedly and I did not envy them: my turn would come.

At the age of fifty. In short, I lost myself without suffering; shaken by sudden panic, I zealously sent in some execrable papers. My grandfather was already frowning; my mother hastened to ask Monsieur Ollivier, my principal teacher, for an appointment. He received us in his small bachelor flat; my mother had put on her musical voice; standing against his arm-chair, I listened to him as I watched the sun through the dusty window-panes. She tried to prove that I was better than my homework: I had learnt to read by myself and I wrote novels. As a final argument, she revealed that I had been a ten-months' child: better cooked than the others, more golden and crisper, for having been longer in the oven. Susceptible to her charms rather than my merits, Monsieur Ollivier listened to her attentively. He was a tall, gaunt man, bald with an expansive cranium, sunken eyes, a waxen complexion, and a few red hairs under his long aquiline nose. He refused to give me private lessons but promised to 'keep an eye' on me. I asked no more: I watched his eyes during lessons; I was sure he was addressing only me; I thought he loved me and that I loved him, and a few kind words did the rest: without trying I became a fairly good pupil. My grandfather used to grumble when he read my end-of-term reports, but he stopped thinking of taking me away from the *lycée*. In the *classe de cinquième*, I had other teachers and lost my privileged treatment; but I had grown used to democracy.

My school work left me no time to write; my new acquaintances took away from me even the urge. At last I had companions! I, the outcast of the public gardens, had been adopted from the first day as if it were the most natural thing in the world: I could not get over it. To tell the truth, my friends seemed closer to me than the young Pardaillans who had broken my heart: they were day-boys, mothers' darlings and studious. No matter: I rejoiced. I led a double life. With my family, I continued to ape the man. But children among themselves detest childish behaviour: they are real men. A man among men, I left the *lycée* every day with the three Malaquins, Jean, René, and André, Paul and Norbert Meyre, Brun, Max

Bercot, and Grégoire, and we would run about and shout in the Place du Panthéon; it was a moment of serious happiness: I washed my hands of the family comedy. Far from wanting to shine, I echoed their laughter, I repeated their catch-phrases and their jokes, kept quiet, obeyed, and imitated my neighbours' gestures. I had but one passion: to identify myself with them. Curt, tough and cheerful, I felt like steel, freed at last from the sin of existing: we used to play ball, between the Hotel des Grands Hommes and the statue of Jean-Jacques Rousseau. I was indispensable: *the right man in the right place*. I no longer felt at all envious of Monsieur Simonnot: to whom would Meyre, feinting towards Grégoire, have passed if *I* had not been *present here now*? How insipid and morbid my dreams of glory seemed beside these lightning intuitions which revealed to me that I was necessary.

Unfortunately, they went out more quickly than they had been lit. According to our mothers, our games 'over-excited' us and sometimes transformed our groups into a small, integral crowd which absorbed me; but we could never forget for long our parents whose invisible presence soon forced us back into the collective loneliness of animal communities. Without aim, end, or hierarchy, our society wavered between complete fusion and juxtaposition. Together we lived in truth, but we could never avoid feeling that we were on loan to each other, and that we each belonged to narrow, powerful and primitive communities which forged fascinating myths, fed on error, and imposed their arbitrary wills on us. Coddled and pious, sensitive, logical, appalled by chaos, hating violence and injustice, united and separated by the tacit conviction that the world had been created for our use and that our respective parents were the best in the world, we were at pains to offend no one and to remain courteous even in our games. Jeers and insults were strictly forbidden; if anyone got carried away, the whole group would surround him, calm him down, and make him beg pardon: his own mother would scold him through the lips of Jean Malaquin or Norbert Meyre. All these ladies were acquainted besides, and were beastly to each other: they passed on our comments and criticisms, and the judgements of each of us on the rest; we, the sons, hid theirs from our companions. My mother returned disgusted from a visit to Madame Malaquin who had told her straight out: 'André thinks that Poulou puts on airs.' This reflection did not bother me: that was how mothers talked among themselves. I felt no resentment towards André and never even mentioned the matter to him. In short, we respected the whole world, rich and poor, soldiers and civilians, young and old, men and beasts: we despised only day-boarders and boarders: they must be very wicked for their families to have abandoned them. Perhaps they had bad parents, but that made no odds: children have the fathers they deserve. In the evenings, after four, when the day-boys had left, the *lycée* became a place full of cut-throats.

Such careful friendships as these cannot avoid a certain coldness. We separated for the holidays without regret. Yet I liked Bercot. The son of a widow, he was like a brother to me. He was good-looking, frail, and gentle. I never tired of looking at his long, black hair arranged in Joan-of-Arc style. But, above all, we were both proud of having read everything, and we would go off on our own into a corner of the covered playground to talk literature: that is to say, to run over for the hundredth time, and always with pleasure, the names of the books which had passed through our hands. One day, he looked at me with the air of a maniac, and confided to me that he wanted to write. I met him later in the top classical form, still good-looking but consumptive: he died at eighteen.

Everyone, including the well-behaved Bercot, admired Bénard, a plump boy susceptible to the cold, who looked like a baby chick. Rumours of his merits had reached our mothers' ears, which annoyed them slightly, but they never wearied of using him as an example: even this did not make us loathe him. That shows how much we liked him. He was a day-boarder and we liked him all the more for it; in our eyes he was an honorary day-boy. In the evenings, under the family lamp, our thoughts would turn to this missionary who remained behind in the jungle to convert the cannibal-boarders and we felt less afraid. It is true to say that even the boarders respected him. I can no longer see very clearly the reasons for this unanimous approval. Bénard was gentle, pleasant, and sensitive; on top of which, he was first in everything. And then his mother made sacrifices for him. Our mothers did not visit this dressmaker, but they often referred to her to make us measure the greatness of maternal love. We thought only of Bénard: he was the torch, the joy in that unfortunate woman's life; we measured the greatness of filial love. In the end, everyone felt sorry for these poor, good people. Yet that would not have been enough: the fact is that Bénard only half-lived; I never saw him without a long woollen scarf; he would smile pleasantly at us but say little and I remember that he had been forbidden to join in our games. Personally, I venerated him all the more because his delicate health separated him from us: he had been put under glass. He used to wave at us and make signs through the window but we did not go near him: we cherished him from afar because he had, in his lifetime, the inconspicuousness of a symbol. Childhood is conformist: we were grateful to him for carrying perfection to impersonality. If he chatted with us, the triviality of his remarks easily delighted us; we never saw him angry or too cheerful; he never raised his hand in class but, when he was asked questions, Truth spoke through his mouth, with no hesitation and no eagerness, as Truth should. He dumbfounded our gang of infant prodigies because he was the best without being prodigious. At that time, we were all more or less fatherless orphans: these Gentlemen were dead or at the front, and those who remained, diminished and emasculated, tried to make their sons forget them; mothers reigned: for us Bénard reflected the negative virtues of this matriarchy.

At the end of the winter, he died. Children and soldiers pay little heed to the dead: yet there were forty of us sobbing behind his coffin. Our mothers watched: the abyss was covered with flowers: they saw to it that we took this departure for a super-school prize awarded during the course of the year. And then Bénard lived so little that he did not really die: he remained with us, a diffuse and sacred presence. Our morality took a step forward: we had our dear departed and we talked of him in whispers, with melancholy pleasure. Perhaps, like him, we too would be carried off before our time: we pictured our mothers' tears and we felt ourselves to be valuable. Yet did I dream all this? I remember only vaguely the hideous reality: this dressmaker, this widow had lost *everything*. Did I really choke with horror at this thought? Did I glimpse Evil, the absence of God, and an uninhabitable world? I think so: otherwise, why should the image of Bénard have retained its painful clarity in my denied, forgotten, lost childhood?

A few weeks later, the *classe de cinquième* A 1 was the scene of a remarkable incident: during the Latin lesson, the door opened, and Bénard came in, accompanied by the porter. He greeted Monsieur Durry, our teacher, and sat down. We recognized his steel spectacles, his muffler, his slightly aquiline nose and his air of a chick susceptible to the cold: I thought God was giving him back to us. Monsieur Durry seemed to share our astonishment: he broke off, breathed heavily and asked: 'Surname, Christian names, day-boy or boarder, parents' profession.' Bénard replied that he was a day-boarder, an engineer's son, and that his name was Paul-Yves Nizan. I was the most astonished of the lot; I spoke to him in break and he responded: a link was formed between us. Yet one detail made me feel that I was dealing not with Bénard but with his satanic double: Nizan squinted. It was too late to take this into account. I had liked, in that face, the incarnation of Good; I ended by liking him for himself. I had been caught in the trap and my leanings to virtue had led me to cherish the Devil. To tell the truth, the pseudo-Bénard was not particularly wicked: he was alive, that was all; he had all the qualities of his double, but they were blighted. In him, Bénard's shyness became deceit. Overcome by violent, passive emotions, he did not shout out, but we saw him turn white with rage, and stammer: what we took for mildness was nothing but a temporary paralysis. It was not truth that issued from his mouth but a sort of cynical and frivolous objectivity which made us uneasy because we were not used to it and, although he worshipped his parents, of course, he was the only one who referred to them ironically. In class, he shone less than Bénard; on the other hand, he had read a lot and wanted to write. In short, he was a complete person, and nothing astonished me more than to see someone who looked like Bénard. Obsessed by the likeness, I never knew if I ought to praise him for the appearance of virtue or blame him for having only its appearance, and I switched endlessly from blind trust to irrational distrust. We became real friends only much later, after a long separation.

For two years, these incidents and these relationships suspended my ruminations without removing their cause. In fact, deep down, nothing had changed: I had stopped thinking about this mandate which had been laid on me under sealed cover by the adults, but it persisted. It took possession of me. When I was nine, I used to keep an eye on myself even in my worst excesses. At ten, I lost sight of myself. I used to run with Brun, and chat with Bercot and Nizan: during this time, my false mission, left to its own devices, took shape and, finally, toppled over in my night; I never saw it again, it made me, it worked its powers of attraction on everything, bending the trees and the walls, and arching the sky above my head. I had thought I was a prince, my madness was to be one. Character-neurosis, says a psychoanalyst friend of mine. He is right: between the summer of 1914 and the autumn of 1916 my mandate became my character; my delirium left my head to flow in my bones.

Nothing new happened to me: I found that what I had acted and prophesied was still intact. One difference only: without consciousness or words, I blindly *realized* everything. Before, I saw my life in images: my death inducing my birth and my birth projecting me towards my death; as soon as I stopped seeing this reciprocity, I became it myself and stretched myself to breaking-point between these two extremes, being born and dying with every heart-beat. My eternity to come became my concrete future: it left its mark on every second of frivolity and it was, at the centre of the deepest concentration, a still deeper absent-mindedness, the emptiness of all plenitude and the trivial unreality of reality; it killed, from a distance, the taste of a caramel in my mouth and the joys and griefs in my heart; but it preserved the emptiest of moments for the sole reason that it would come at last and that it brought me nearer to it; it gave me the patience to live: never again did I want to jump twenty years or run through another twenty; never again did I imagine the far-off days of my triumph; I waited. Each minute, I waited for the next because it brought with it the one which followed. I lived serenely in a state of extreme urgency: always in front of myself, everything absorbed me but nothing held me back. What a relief! Before, my days were so alike that I sometimes wondered if I were not condemned to an eternal repetition of the same one. They had not changed much, they still kept the bad habit of sinking away; but *I*, I had changed in them: it was no longer time which ebbed across my motionless childhood; it was myself, an arrow fired by order, which was making a hole in time and flying straight to its goal. In 1948, at Utrecht, Professor Van Lennep showed me some aptitude tests. One card in particular caught my interest: on it was depicted a horse at the gallop, a man walking, an eagle in full flight, and a motor boat springing forward; the person tested had to point to the drawing which gave him the greatest impression of speed. I said: 'It's the boat.' Then I looked curiously at the drawing which had impressed itself on me so strongly: the boat seemed to have detached itself from the lake, and in a moment would be gliding above that rippling swamp. The reason for my choice came to me immediately: when I was ten I had had the impression that my prow was cleaving the present and wrenching me away from it; since which time I have been running, am still running. Speed is conveyed, to my eyes, less by the distance covered in a specific lapse of time than by its wrenching power.

More than twenty years ago, one evening as he was crossing the Place d'Italie, Giacometti was knocked down by a car. Injured, his leg twisted, he was at first aware, in the lucid faint into which he fell, of a kind of joy: 'At last something's happening to me!' I appreciate his radical attitude: he expected the worst; this life which he loved to the point of never wanting any other had been upset, perhaps smashed by the stupid violence of chance: 'So,' he thought, 'I wasn't born to be a sculptor or even to live; I was born for nothing.' What excited him was the menacing order of causes suddenly unmasked and imposing on the lights of the city, on men, and on his own body, flattened in the mud, the paralysing aspect of a disaster: to a sculptor, the Kingdom of the mineral world is never far off. I admire this will to welcome everything. If you like surprises, you must like them to this extreme; even to those rare lightning-flashes which reveal to its lovers that the earth was not created for them.

At the age of ten, I asserted that they were the only things I did like. Every link in my life must be unexpected and smell of fresh paint. I agreed in advance to reverses and misfortunes and, in all fairness, it must be said that I put a good face on them. One evening the electricity went out: a power-failure. Someone in the room called me, and I walked forward with my arms out, hitting my head so hard against a door jamb that I broke a tooth. This amused me and, in spite of the pain, I laughed at it. Just as Giacometti was to laugh later on over his leg, but for diametrically opposite reasons. Since I had decided in advance that my story would have a happy ending, the unexpected could only be a catch, the novelty an appearance; people's needs, by causing me to be born, had determined everything: I saw that broken tooth as a sign, an obscure warning that I would understand later on. In other words, I preserved the order of ends in all circumstances and at all costs; I was looking at my life through my death and saw only a closed memory which nothing could leave and nothing could enter. Can my sense of security be imagined? Risks did not exist: I had to deal only with their accidental counterfeits. The newspapers seemed to suggest that scattered forces loitered about the streets, and struck down ordinary people: but I, pre-destined, would never meet any of them. I might lose an arm, a leg, or both eyes. But everything was according to plan: my adversities would never be anything but tests or the means of writing a book. I learned to bear grief and sickness: in them I saw the beginning of my triumphal death, the steps it was cutting to raise me to itself. This somewhat brutal concern did not displease me and I was anxious to show myself worthy of it. I accepted the worst as the condition of the best; even my mistakes had their uses, which was the same as saying that I made none. At ten, I was sure of myself: modest and insufferable, I saw in my discomfitures the conditions of my posthumous victory. Blind or legless, misled by my errors, I would win the war by dint of losing battles. I did not distinguish between the tests reserved for the elect and the setbacks for which I bore the responsibility; this means that, deep down, I saw my crimes as adversities and claimed my misfortune as mistakes. Actually, I could not catch an infection, whether it was measles or a cold in the head, without pleading guilty: I had not been careful enough or I had forgotten to wear my overcoat or my scarf. I have always preferred to accuse myself rather than the universe; not out of good nature: but to remain my own master. This arrogance did not exclude humility: I was all the more willing to think I was fallible because my failings were necessarily the shortest route to Good. I contrived it so that I felt, in the movement of my life, an irresistible urge which forced me without ceasing, even in spite of myself, to take new steps forward.

All children know that they are progressing. They are not allowed to be unaware of it, either: 'Progress to be made, in progress, serious and steady progress. . . .' The grown-ups used to tell us the History of France: after the first Republic, which was dubious, there was the second and then the third, which was the good one: never two without three. Middle-class optimism at that time was summed up in the programme of the Radicals; growing material abundance, suppression of poverty by the multiplication of enlightenment and small properties. It had been put within the reach of us young Gentlemen and we discovered with satisfaction that our individual progress reflected that of the Nation. Yet those who wished to raise themselves above their fathers were rare: for most of them, all they wanted was to reach manhood; afterwards, they would stop growing and developing: it was the world about them which would grow better and more comfortable spontaneously. Some of us were waiting for this moment with impatience, others with fear, still others with regret. As for me, before I became dedicated I grew up in indifference: I did not give a damn for the *toga praetexta*. My grandfather thought that I was tiny and grieved over it: 'He'll have the build of a Sartre,' my grandmother used to say to annoy him. He would pretend not to hear, plant himself in front of me, and look me up and down: 'He's growing!' he would eventually say, without much conviction. I shared neither his hopes nor his anxieties: weeds grow, too; proof that you can become tall without growing in goodness. My problem, then, was to be good *in aeternum*. Everything changed when my life gathered speed: it was no longer enough to do well, I had to do *better* the whole time. I had but one law: to climb. To feed my pretensions and to conceal their excess, I turned to common experience: in the faltering advances of my childhood I wanted to see the first effects of my destiny. These genuine but small and very ordinary improvements gave me the illusion of testing my climbing powers. A public child, I adopted, in public, the myth of my class and generation: people make use of what has been acquired and capitalize experience, and the present is enriched by the whole of the past. In private, I was far from satisfied with it. I could not admit that a person received his being from outside, that it maintained itself through inertia, or that the movements of the soul were the result of previous movements. Born of a future expectation, I leapt about, complete and shining, for ever repeating the ceremony of my birth: in the affections of my heart, I wanted to see the crackling of sparks. How then would the past have enriched me? It had not created me; it was I, on the contrary, rising from my ashes, who was tearing my fame from nothingness by my continually renewed creation. I was reborn better and I used the inert reserves of my soul better for the simple reason that death, each time closer, lit me up more brightly with its obscure light. I was often told: the past drives us forward, but I was convinced that it was the future which was drawing me on; I would have loathed to feel in me forces docile to the working, the slow blossoming of my abilities. I had stuffed my soul with the middle-class idea of continual progress and I was making an internal combustion engine of it; I humbled the past in favour of the present and the present in favour of the future; I was transforming a calm process of evolution into a revolutionary and intermittent process of disaster. Some years ago, it was pointed out to me that the characters in my plays and novels make their decisions suddenly and in crises – that, for instance, it takes only a moment for Orestes in *Les Mouches* to achieve his conversion. By Jove: that is because I make them in my own image; not as I am, I dare say, but as I have wanted to be.

I became a traitor and I have remained one. In vain I have put myself wholly into what I undertake or given myself unreservedly to work, anger, or friendship; in a moment, I shall deny myself. I know this, and want it and I am already betraying myself, in the heat of passion, by the joyful anticipation of my future betrayal. On the whole, I honour my commitments as well as the next man; constant in my affections and my behaviour, I am unfaithful to my emotions: there was a time when the last monument, picture, or landscape I had seen was the most beautiful; I displeased my friends by referring cynically or frivolously – to convince myself that I was detached from them – to common memories which had, perhaps, remained precious to them. Not liking myself enough, I ran away forwards; result: I like myself still less, and this inexorable advance continually disqualifies me in my own eyes: yesterday I acted badly because it was yesterday and I am aware today of the harsh judgement I shall pass on myself tomorrow. No promiscuity, though: I keep my past at a respectful distance. Adolescence, maturity, even the year that has just passed will always be the Old Régime: the New is heralded at the present hour but is never instituted: tomorrow never comes. I have struck out my earliest years, in particular: when I began this book, it took me a lot of time to decipher them beneath the crossings-out. Friends remarked in astonishment, when I was thirty: 'You seem as if you never had any parents. Or childhood.' And I was stupid enough to feel flattered. Yet I like and respect the humble and dogged loyalty that some people – especially women – preserve for their tastes, their desires, their former concerns and vanished festivals, and I admire their determination to remain the same amid change, to safeguard their memories, and to take a first doll, a milk-tooth or an early love with them to their graves. I have known men who late in life have slept

148

with an old woman for the simple reason that they desired her in their youth; others harbour resentment against the dead or would fight rather than admit to some trivial mistake they made twenty years earlier. I bear no resentments and I obligingly confess everything: I have a flair for self-criticism, provided it is not foisted on me. Unpleasant things were done in 1936 and 1945 to the person who bore my name: does that concern me? I post slights endured to his debit: this fool did not even know how to make himself respected. An old friend meets me; a long tale of bitterness: he has been nursing a grievance for seventeen years; on one particular occasion, I treated him without consideration. I vaguely remember that I defended myself, at the time, by counter-attacking, that I reproached him for his touchiness and persecution mania – in short, that I have my own private version of the incident: so I am all the more anxious to adopt his; I agree with him, and heap blame on myself. I behaved conceitedly and selfishly, I am heartless. It is a cheerful massacre: I am delighted with my lucidity; to recognize my mistakes with such good grace is to prove to myself that I could never make them again. Would you believe it? My loyalty, my generous confession merely irritate the plaintiff. He has foiled me, but he knows I am using him: he resents me, the living me, present or past, *the same person* he has always known, and I am leaving him with my cast-off slough for the pleasure of feeling that I am *a new-born babe*. Eventually, it is my turn to get annoyed with this fanatic for raking up the dead. Inversely, if I am reminded of some occasion out of which, I am told, I did not come too badly, I brush aside the memory; they think I am being modest but it is quite the contrary: I think that I should do better today and *very much* better tomorrow. Mature writers do not like to be congratulated too enthusiastically on their earliest work: but I am sure that it is to me that such compliments give the least pleasure. My best book is the one I am busy writing; immediately after that comes the one most recently published, but I am getting ready, quietly, to loathe it soon afterwards. If the critics find it bad today, they may possibly wound me, but in six months I shall not be far from sharing their opinion. On one condition, though: however poor and worthless they consider this work, I want them to rate it above everything that I have done before it; I am willing for the lot to be totally disparaged provided the chronological hierarchy is maintained, the only thing which gives me the chance of doing better tomorrow, still better the day after and of ending with a masterpiece.

Naturally I am not taken in: I am aware that we repeat ourselves. But this most recently acquired knowledge gnaws at my old established facts without entirely dispelling them. My life has a few severe critics who let me get away with nothing; they often catch me falling into the same ruts again. They tell me so, I believe them and, then, at the last moment, I congratulate myself: yesterday I was blind; today I have progressed because I have realized that I am progressing no longer. Sometimes, I am my own witness for the prosecution. For instance, it occurs to me that, two years ago, I wrote a page which might be of use to me. I look for it but cannot find it; so much the better: I was about to succumb to laziness and slip an old thing into a new work: I write so much better today; I shall redo it. When I have finished, as chance would have it, I find the missing page again. Amazing: I expressed the same idea in the same way, almost to a comma. I hesitate and then I throw the obsolete document into the waste-paper basket and keep the new version: it is just that much better than the old one. In a word, I compromise; in my disillusion, I cheat myself in order to feel, once again, in spite of the ravages of age, the youthful intoxication of the mountaineer.

When I was ten, I was not yet aware of my manias and repetitions, and doubt never crossed my mind: trotting along, chattering, fascinated by what was going on in the street, I never stopped renewing my skin and I could hear the old skins falling one on top of the other. When I went back up the rue Soufflot, I felt at each step, as the dazzling rows of shop-windows went by, the movement of my life, its law and the noble mandate of being unfaithful to everything. I was taking my whole self along with me. My grandmother wanted to match her dinner service; I went with her into a glass and china shop; she pointed to a soup-tureen, with a red apple on top of its lid, and to some flowered plates. It was not quite what she wanted: there were flowers on the plates, of course, but also some brown insects climbing up the stems. It was the shop-keeper's turn to brighten: she knew exactly what the customer wanted, she used to have it, but they stopped making it three years ago; this was a more recent model, better value, and then, with or without insects, flowers were still flowers, weren't they, no one was going to look for the little creature, you must admit. My grandmother did not agree; she kept on: couldn't they have a look in the stockroom? Ah, yes, of course, in the stockroom. But that would take time and the shopkeeper was on her own: her assistant had just left her. I had been consigned to a corner, with a warning to touch nothing. I was forgotten, terrified by the fragile objects around me with their dusty sheen, Pascal's death mask and a chamber-pot decorated with the head of President Fallières. Now, in spite of appearances, I was a bogus supporting player. In the same way, some authors push small part players to the front of the stage and present their hero receding off stage.

But the reader is not deceived: he has run through the last chapter to see if the novel has a happy ending, and he knows that the pale young man, against the fireplace, has three hundred and fifty pages in the womb. Three hundred and fifty pages of love and adventure. I had at least five hundred. I was the hero of a long story with a happy ending. I had stopped telling myself this story: what was the use? I felt romantic, that was all. Time was dragging backwards the puzzled old ladies, the china flowers and the whole shop; the black shirts were fading; the voices were getting woolly; I felt sorry for my grandmother; she would certainly not be appearing in the second part. But I was the beginning, the middle and the end all rolled into one small boy, already old, already dead, *here*, in the shadows, between the stacks of plates higher than himself, and *outside*, very far away, in the vast and gloomy sunshine of glory. I was the particle at the beginning of its trajectory and the series of waves which flows back on it after it has struck the terminal buffer. Reassembled and compressed, one hand on my tomb and the other on my cradle, I felt brief and splendid, a flash of lightning swallowed up in darkness.

Yet boredom did not leave me; sometimes it was unobtrusive and sometimes nauseating and when I could no longer stand it I would succumb to the deadliest temptation. Orpheus lost Eurydice through impatience; I often lost myself through impatience. Led astray by idleness, I would sometimes turn back to my folly when I should have ignored it, kept it under my thumb and fixed my attention on external objects; at such times, I wanted to *realize* myself straight away and embrace at one glance the totality which haunted me when I was not thinking about it. Disaster! Progress, optimism, cheerful betrayals and the secret end – all collapsed because of what I had myself added to Madame Picard's prediction. The prediction remained but what could I do about it? From the wish to preserve every one of my moments, this empty oracle would not distinguish any single one of them. The future, withered at a blow, was nothing but a shell; I reverted to the problems of my existence and realized that they had never left me.

A memory without a date: I am sitting on a bench in the Luxembourg Gardens: Anne-Marie has begged me to sit down beside her because I have been running too much and I am drenched with sweat. At least, that is the order of causes. I am so bored that I am arrogant enough to reverse it: I have run because I *had* to be drenched with sweat, so that my mother would have the opportunity of calling me back. Everything led to that bench; everything had to lead to it. What is its role? I do not know and at first I do not care: not one of the impressions which are skimming past me will be lost; there is a goal: I shall know it; my nephews will know it. I am swinging my short legs which do not reach the ground; I see a man going by carrying a parcel, and a hunchbacked woman: that will do, I keep saying to myself in a trance: 'It is absolutely essential that I remain seated.' My boredom redoubles: I no longer try to avoid risking a glance inside myself: I am not asking for sensational revelations but I would like to guess at the meaning of this moment, feel its urgency and enjoy something of that obscure, vital prescience which I associate with Musset and

Hugo. Naturally, I see only mists. The abstract postulation that I am necessary and the crude intuition of my existence dwell side by side, neither warring nor mingling. I can think of nothing but running off and retrieving the dull speed which bore me away; in vain: the spell is broken. I have pins and needles in the bends of my knees, and I wriggle. Most opportunely, Heaven entrusts me with a new mission: it is absolutely essential for me to start running again. I jump down and run at full speed; at the end of the path, I turn round: nothing has moved; nothing has happened. I hide my disappointment from myself in words: in a furnished room at Aurillac, I aver, round about 1945, this race will have inestimable consequences. I confess that I am overcome and I grow excited: I pretend to trust in the Holy Ghost, to force his hand: in my frenzy, I swear that I will deserve the chance which he has given me. Everything is skin-deep, everything is played on the nerves, and I know it. My mother has already pounced on me, here's your woollen jersey, your muffler, your overcoat: I let myself be wrapped up, I am a parcel. Once again I have to endure the rue Soufflot, the moustache of Monsieur Trigon the *concierge*, and the wheezings of the hydraulic lift. Finally, the calamitous little pretender is back in the library; he drags himself from one chair to another, turns the pages of some of the books and rejects them. I go over to the window, spot a fly under the curtain, corner it in a muslin trap and direct a murderous forefinger at it. This moment is not in the programme; it is a part of common time, set aside, incomparable, motionless, and nothing will come of it either this evening or later on: Aurillac will remain for ever unaware of the blurred eternity. Humanity is drowsing; as for the famous writer – a saint, who would not harm a fly – he has just gone out. Alone and futureless in a stagnating moment, a child is asking for powerful sensations from murder; since I am refused the destiny of a man, I shall be the destiny of a fly. I am in no hurry, I give it time to take in the giant leaning over it. I push my finger forward: it bursts and I am foiled! Good God, there was no need to kill it! In the whole of creation, it was the only being that was afraid of me; I no longer matter to anyone. Insecticide, I take the victim's place and become an insect in my turn. I am a fly and have always been one. This time I have touched bottom. There is nothing for me to do except pick up *Les Aventures du capitaine Corcoran* from the table, drop down on the carpet and open at random the oft-read book; I feel so weary and sad that I am no longer conscious of my nerves and, from the first line, I forget myself. Corcoran is stalking his prey in the empty library; his rifle under his arm and his tigress at his heels. The jungle thickets hastily take up their positions around them; in the distance I have planted some trees, and monkeys are leaping from branch to branch. Suddenly, Louison, the tigress, starts to growl and Corcoran stands immobile: it is the enemy. This is the thrilling moment which my glory chooses to return to its abode. Humanity wakes with a start and calls me to its aid, and the Holy Ghost whispers these shattering words: 'You would not be looking for me if you had not found me.' These blandishments will be in vain; there is no one here to listen to them except the valiant Corcoran. The Famous Writer, as if he had been waiting only for this declaration, re-enters: a great-nephew is bending his fair head over the story of my life, his eyes are moist with tears, the future is dawning, infinite love wraps me about, and lights gyrate in my heart. I do not stir or glance at the show. I carry on my reading like a good boy, the lights eventually go out and all I can feel is a rhythm, an irresistible urge. I am unmoored, I am moving forward and the engine is purring. I experience the speed of my soul.

This was my beginning: I was running away; external forces shaped my flight and made me. Religion showed through an outmoded concept of culture and served as a model: because it is childish, nothing touches a child more closely. I was taught Bible history, the Gospel and the catechism without being given the means of believing: the result was a disorder which became my private order. There were some puckers and a considerable shift; levied on Catholicism, the sacred settled into Belles-Lettres and the writer appeared, an *ersatz* of the Christian I could not be: his only concern was salvation, the one aim of his stay here below was to earn for himself posthumous bliss through trials endured worthily. Death was reduced to a transitory rite and earthly immortality presented itself as a substitute for eternal life. To reassure myself that the human race would perpetuate me it was agreed in my mind that it would not come to an end. To extinguish myself in it was to be born and to become infinite, but if anyone had advanced the theory in front of me that some cataclysm might one day destroy the planet, even fifty thousand years hence, I would have been terrified. Today, in my disillusion, I still cannot envisage the cooling of the sun without fear: it matters little to me if my fellow-creatures forget me the day after my burial; while they live, I shall haunt them, elusive, nameless, present in each one like the thousands of millions of dead of whom I know nothing and yet whom I preserve from annihilation. But should humanity ever disappear, it will kill off its dead for good.

The myth was a very simple one and I swallowed it without difficulty. Protestant and Catholic, my twin denominational adherence preserved me from believing in the Saints, the Virgin and eventually in God while they were still called by their names. But a vast collective power had penetrated me; lodged in my heart, it was keeping watch, it was the Faith of others. It is enough to debaptize and modify superficially its normal object: faith recognized it beneath the disguises which deceived me, threw itself on it and enclosed it in its tendrils. I thought I was giving myself to Literature when I was, in fact, taking holy orders. In me the certainty of the humblest believer became the proud evidence of my predestination. Why not predestined? Is not every Christian one of the elect? I grew up, a rank weed, on the compost-heap of catholicity; my roots sucked up its juices, and from them I made my sap. This was the cause of that lucid blindness from which I suffered for thirty years. One morning, in 1917, at La Rochelle, I was waiting for some companions who were supposed to accompany me to the *lycée*; they were late. Soon I could think of nothing more to distract myself, and I decided to think about the Almighty. He at once tumbled down into the blue sky and vanished without explanation: He does not exist, I said to myself, in polite astonishment, and I thought the matter was settled. In one sense it was, because I have never since had the least temptation to revive Him. But the Other, the Invisible, the Holy Ghost, he who guaranteed my mandate and dominated my life through great, anonymous, and sacred forces, he remained. I had all the more trouble freeing myself from him because he had lodged himself in the back of my head among the made-up notions I used to understand, place, and justify myself. For a long time, writing was asking Death or Religion in disguise to tear my life away from chance. I was of the Church. As a militant, I wanted to save myself through works; as a mystic, I tried to unveil the stillness of existence through a counteracting murmur of words, and, above all, I confused things with their names: that is belief. I was dim of sight. As long as that lasted, I was out of trouble. I pulled off this noble achievement at that age of thirty: describing in *La Nausée* – most sincerely, I can assure you – the unjustified, brackish existence of my fellow-creatures and vindicating my own. I *was* Roquentin; in him I exposed, without self-satisfaction, the web of my life; at the same time I was *myself*, the elect, the chronicler of hells, and a photomicroscope of glass and steel bent over my own protoplasmic juices. Later on, I cheerfully demonstrated that man is impossible; impossible myself, I differed from others only in this one mandate: I had to illustrate this impossibility which, suddenly, was transfigured and became my most intimate potentiality, the object of my mission and the springboard of my glory. I was prisoner of these evidences, but I did not see them: I saw the world through them. Mystified and a fraud to my very bones, I cheerfully wrote about our wretched lot. In my dogmatism, I doubted everything except that I had been chosen by doubt; I was restoring with one hand what I destroyed with the other and I took anxiety as the proof of my safety; I was happy.

I have changed. I will describe later what acids ate into the distorting transparencies which wrapped me round, and how and when I became apprenticed to violence and discovered my ugliness – which was for a long while my negative principle, the quicklime in which the wonderful child was dissolved – why I came to think systematically against myself to the point of weighing the evidence for an idea by how much I disliked it.

My retrospective illusions are in pieces. Martyrdom, salvation, immortality: all are crumbling; the building is falling in ruins. I have caught the Holy Ghost in the cellars and flung him out of them. Atheism is a cruel, long-term business: I believe I have gone through it to the end. I see clearly, I am free from illusions, I know my real tasks, and I must surely deserve a civic prize; for about ten years I have been a man who is waking up, cured of a long, bitter-sweet madness, who cannot get away from it, who cannot recall his old ways without laughing and who no longer has any idea what to do with his life. I have become once again the traveller without a ticket that I was at seven: the ticket-inspector has entered my compartment and is looking at me, but less sternly than he once did: in fact, all he wants is to go away, and let me complete the journey in peace; as long as I give him valid excuse of some kind, he will be satisfied. Unfortunately I cannot find one and, besides, do not even want to look for one: we shall go on talking together, ill at ease, as far as Dijon where I know quite well that no one is waiting for me.

I have renounced my vocation, but I have not unfrocked myself. I still write. What else can I do?

Nulla dies sine linea.

It is my habit and it is also my profession. For a long while I treated my pen as a sword: now I realize how helpless we are. It does not matter: I am writing, I shall write books; they are needed; they have a use all the same. Culture saves nothing and nobody, nor does it justify. But it is a product of man: he projects himself through it and recognizes himself in it; this critical mirror alone shows him his image. For the real, this old ruined house, my imposture, is also my character: you can get rid of a neurosis but you are never cured of yourself. All the characteristics of the child, worn, defaced, humiliated, huddled in a corner and passed over in silence, have survived in the fifty-year-old man. Most of the time they flatten themselves in the shadows, they watch: at the first sign of inattention, they lift their heads and move into broad daylight in some form of disguise: I claim sincerely to write only for my own time, but I am troubled by my present notoriety: it is not glory because I am alive and that is enough to give the lie to my old dreams; could it be that I still nurse them secretly? Not quite: I have, I think, adapted them: since I have lost the chance of dying unknown, I sometimes flatter myself that I live misunderstood. Griselda is not dead. Pardaillan lives on in me. And Strogoff. I depend only on those who depend only on God, and I do not believe in God. Try and sort this out. Personally I cannot, and I sometimes wonder if I am not playing at loser takes all and if I am doing my best to trample on my hopes of other days so that everything will be rendered to me a hundredfold. In that case, I would be Philoctetes: magnificent and stinking, this sick man gave away even his bow without any condition; but you can be sure that, underneath, he expected his reward.

Enough of that. Mamie would say:

'*Glissez, mortels, n'appuyez pas.*'

What I like about my madness is that it has safeguarded me, from the very first, against the blandishments of 'the elite': I have never seen myself as the happy owner of a 'talent': my one concern was to save myself – nothing in my hands, nothing in my pockets – through work and faith. Now at last my unadulterated choice did not set me up above anyone: with neither tools nor equipment, I gave my entire self to the task of saving my entire self. If I put away Salvation among the stage properties as impossible, what is left? A whole man, made of all men, worth all of them, and any one of them worth him.

MORE ABOUT PENGUINS, PELICANS
AND PUFFINS

For further information about books available from Penguins please write to Dept EP, Penguin Books Ltd, Harmondsworth, Middlesex UB7 0DA.

In the U.S.A.: For a complete list of books available from Penguins in the United States write to Dept DG, Penguin Books, 299 Murray Hill Parkway, East Rutherford, New Jersey 07073.

In Canada: For a complete list of books available from Penguins in Canada write to Penguin Books Canada Limited, 2801 John Street, Markham, Ontario L3R 1B4.

In Australia: For a complete list of books available from Penguins in Australia write to the Marketing Department, Penguin Books Australia Ltd, P.O. Box 257, Ringwood, Victoria 3134.

In New Zealand: For a complete list of books available from Penguins in New Zealand write to the Marketing Department, Penguin Books (N.Z.) Ltd, Private Bag, Takapuna, Auckland 9.

In India: For a complete list of books available from Penguins in India write to Penguin Overseas Ltd, 706 Eros Apartments, 56 Nehru Place, New Delhi 110019.

ROADS TO FREEDOM

Sartre's famous trilogy

THE AGE OF REASON

This novel covers two days in the life of Mathieu Delarue, a teacher of philosophy, and in the lives of his acquaintances and friends. Individual tragedies and happiness are etched against the Paris summer of 1938, with its night clubs, galleries, students, and café society.

But behind it all there is a threat, only half realized at the time, of the coming catastrophe of the Second World War.

'Constantly delights with its brilliance' – *Spectator*

'A dynamic, deeply disturbing novel' – Elizabeth Bowen.

THE REPRIEVE

The Reprieve follows *The Age of Reason* and includes many of the characters of the first book. It surveys that heat-wave week in September 1938, when Europe waited tensely for the result of the Munich conference. Sartre's technique of almost simultaneous description of several scenes enables him to suggest the mood of all Europe as it tried hard to blinker itself against the threat of war.

'His method is consummately able. It is only a writer with an exquisite sense of rhythm who can mix episode with episode as M. Sartre does here' – *Observer*

IRON IN THE SOUL

This was the meaning of defeat. Day by day, hour by hour, this is what men thought, felt and did, as France fell. Men who shrugged, men who ran, and brave men like Mathieu who learned to hate and kill. The third volume of *Roads to Freedom*.